While God has chosen the foolishness of preaching to save those who believe, each generation throughout church history has had to move with the technology of the times and use it to reach the lost. I thank God for Craig von Buseck's willingness, not only to move with the times, but also for his vision to help other to do the same. May God bless *NetCasters* and greatly use it to catch men.

—**Ray Comfort**, Way of the Master

NetCasters serves as both a call to effectively utilize Internet technology for evangelism and a road map of how to do that. I appreciate Craig's heart for the Gospel and his grasp of the many opportunities for Christians to share their faith online.

—**Dr. Sterling Huston**
Chairman, Executive Committee
Internet Evangelism Network

NetCasters presents a unique overview into the vast and growing potential of the digital media to share the good news of Jesus. It's well-researched and visionary coverage, interviews and case studies are indispensable to anyone needing to understand the nature of the new media and how to use them effectively.

—**Tony Whittaker**, coordinator of Internet Evangelism Day

As I read *NetCasters* this line lodged in my mind and wouldn't let me go, "The Internet is ripe, but the laborers are few". The stories are compelling, and even his introduction to digital technology understandable for nontechies like me. I believe this book will convince many to become "netcasters". Count me in, Craig!

—**Lon Allison**, Executive Director
Billy Graham Center, Wheaton College

Craig von Buseck takes you to a place that every church must now consider as part of their growth and discipleship outreach. The white for harvest field today is the desktop, the laptop, the cell phone . . . the network. This book contains strategic advice, excellent examples, valuable contacts, and how to think about getting started as a NetCaster in this emerging digital world.

—**Walt Wilson**, Founder and Chairman of
Global Media Outreach

In *NetCasters*, Craig von Buseck delivers a sobering but exciting truth. The future of evangelism lies not in sending missionaries to every corner of the globe but delivering the gospel message through the Internet to a world crazy over online media. *NetCasters* serves as a highly useful guide for the next generation of evangelists.

—**Chris Carpenter**, Director of Internet Programming, CBN.com

Craig von Buseck had me from the first few pages. I couldn't put the book down. More than just demographics and projections, NetCasters is practical, connected, and forward directed. I highly recommend this book to anyone interested in communicating Jesus Christ to our ever-developing new world. It is a must read.

—**David Bruce**, Webmaster HollywoodJesus.com

Craig has managed to capture, as a snapshot in time, the one church in the middle of the most awesome moment in history—the fulfillment of the Great Commission of Jesus Christ on its primary mission field of the twenty-first century! Craig unfolds the road map of the church's travels on today's Roman roads of Search, Social Media, Metaverses, and more on all devices in all places. Watch God move cynics, skeptics, seekers, and believers from looking for information to joining online social communities that interact and disciple in real time at the speed of light! I recommend this book—without reservation!

—**Greg Outlaw**, Volunteer President & CEO,
AllAboutGOD.com Ministries, Inc.

The Internet has been compared to an old spaghetti western. It contains the good, the bad, and the ugly. *NetCasters* should be read by every Christian desiring to increase the good by sharing the good news of salvation on the internet.

—**Bill Gordon**, North American Mission Board of the Southern
Baptist Convention

NetCasters is a very complete and practical overview of how to go about Christian ministry on the Internet. It is well-researched, biblical, practical and passionate and strikes the right balance between wonderful storytelling and technical information. I thoroughly recommend *NetCasters* to anyone who wants to use computers and the Internet to facilitate the Great Commission.

—**John Edmiston**, Chairman/CEO Cybermissions

This book will help everyone understand the mechanics of being a NetCaster. It communicates the opportunity we have to use the collection of communication media we call "the internet" to engage people in eternal conversations. Profiles of Netcaster heroes and the liberal quoting of wisdom show how God is calling people from all walks of life to engage in the greatest communication opportunity of all time.

—**Keith Seabourn,** Chief Technology Officer
Campus Crusade for Christ

Craig con Buseck's book *NetCasters* is a valuable resource for those wanting to learn more about using digital means to spread the gospel around the world. Craig trumpets a clear call to the church and provides her with a wealth of resources to take advantage of modern technology to further God's kingdom. I heartily recommend it!

—**Frank Johnson**
StrategicDigitalOutreach.com

Netcasters presents compelling research that shows how the Internet can help us reach communities more concerned with authenticity and relationships than media hype and traditional marketing. With a mix of real-world testimonies, meticulous analysis and actual recommendations, Craig presents readers with a guidebook for reaching people in the digital generation. Craig helps to navigate the growing the world of online communication and shows not only how to use it—but tells us why we need to.

—**Jesse Carey,** CBN.com Blogger, Social Media Manager, and
former editor of RelevantMagazine.com

Truly a man ahead of his time, Craig von Buseck is to Internet evangemlism, what Bill Gates was to Web site navigation.

—**Allison Bottke,** author of *Setting Boundaries with Your Adult Children* and the founder of BoomerBabesRock.com Web site and blog

There's never been a more exciting time to proclaim the life-changing good news of Jesus Christ to the nations. My hat's off to Craig von Buseck for making Internet evangelism come alive in this powerful new book. Highly recommended!

—**David Sanford,** award-winning author and executive editor of the
acclaimed *Holy Bible: Mosaic,* www.HolyBibleMosaic.com

We need to redeem technology and use it for God's purposes. This book will give you fresh perspective on how we can do that.

—**Mark Batterson,** Lead Pastor,
National Community Church, Washington, D.C.

The future is in your hands—literally. NetCasters outlines the next wave of reaching millions of people with the good news of the gospel. This comprehensive process is made easy with Craig as your guide. You will rapidly learn how to join the "NetCasters Revolution" and be part of using the Internet for good to change lives one heart at a time.

—**Dwight Bain**
Nationally Certified Counselor, Life Coach and Author

Finally a book that spearheads the evangelism opportunity Christians have when utilizing the power of the internet as an effective way to reach others for Christ.

—**Jerome Mark Mikulich**
3CordMarketing.net

"People do their secret thinking on the Internet," says John Edmiston, quoted in Craig Von Buseck's excellent book, *NetCasters*. That simple but profound statement opens us to why millions are searching the Web for answers to their spiritual questions. The collected information in *NetCasters* is so valuable I wish every church and ministry leader could read it—and bring their evangelism efforts into greater fruitfulness in this digital era.

—**Rev. David R Hackett**
Associate Director, visionSynergy

Are you committed to finding new ways to reach lost people in the shifting sands of today's global culture? If so, read *NetCasters*! Craig von Busek has written a comprehensive guide to how the Internet is (and often is not) being used to further the kingdom. Woven throughout his well-researched material are compelling stories of how God is using technology to reach the most unlikely candidates. *NetCasters* calls attention to this vast harvest, rightly challenging the church to repent of apathy and use every digital means to communicate Christ's love. Additionally, *NetCasters* provides practical suggestions the reader can implement immediately to expand his or her impact for Christ with a just few keystrokes and mouse clicks.

—**Christy Talbert**
YFC Online Corrdinator, Central Ohio Youth for Christ

NET CASTERS

USING THE INTERNET TO
MAKE FISHERS OF MEN

NET
CASTERS

USING THE INTERNET TO
MAKE FISHERS OF MEN

CRAIG VON BUSECK

B&H
PUBLISHING GROUP

NASHVILLE, TENNESSEE

978-0-8054-4784-2

Published by B&H Publishing Group
Nashville, Tennessee

Dewey Decimal Classification: 269.2
Subject Heading: INTERNET IN EVANGELISTIC WORK \
INTERNET—RELIGIOUS ASPECTS—CHRISTIANITY

Unless otherwise noted, all Scripture is from the
Holman Christian Bible® Copyright © 1999, 2000, 2002,
2003, 2009 by Holman Bible Publishers. Used by permission.

At the time of the printing,
all Web sites were checked for accuracy.

1 2 3 4 5 6 7 8 • 14 13 12 11 10

DEDICATION

To my father, Clemens von Buseck—a beacon of God's light, leading our family and countless others to safety in the harbor of Jesus' love.

CONTENTS

Foreword

There's a part of me that always cringes when I see a new book or article on evangelism. Not because it isn't an important topic, but because I think we as followers of Christ have had the tendency down through the years to look for exciting methods or new technologies rather than faithfully heeding the command of Scripture to share our faith. Innovation is not a replacement for obedience.

That simple caveat out of the way, I am excited that Craig has chosen to address the opportunities of digital evangelism, and I appreciate the comprehensive way in which he approaches the subject. Having spent the last fifteen years of my life working with churches and ministry organizations around the world to help them understand how to use Internet technologies to fulfill the purposes to which God has called them, I'm convinced that these new "tools" offer a great opportunity for the gospel.

I think it is important to keep a couple of things in mind as you read this book. First, Internet evangelism is not for everybody. This is not a tool that replaces other means of evangelism, and I hope you don't read Craig's stirring call to become a "NetCaster" as endorsing digital evangelism as the only, or even the best, means to reach people with the good news of Jesus Christ.

The Great Commission that Jesus gave to His disciples (and to us) can be summarized this way—"as you are going . . . make disciples." In other words, wherever your life takes you, you are an ambassador of Jesus Christ and an agent of reconciliation. *Wherever you are, be there with the gospel.* If you have never used the Internet before, then this tool may not be for you. But if your daily life takes you into the world of the Internet (whether on Facebook, with a personal blog, through e-mail or in any of a dozen other ways), then it is your duty as a follower of Christ to live your life authentically in front of a watching world and to look for ways to share the life that you have found in Him.

My second reminder would be that it is very important that we not fall in love with a particular technology rather than falling in love with sharing our faith. Technologies come and go. Different situations call for different tools, and a workman with only one tool in his toolbox is very limited in the scope of needs that he or she can address. That having been said, the Internet and other digital technologies can be great tools for seeing people come into a saving relationship with Jesus Christ.

I pray that many people will catch a vision for how God can use them in online evangelism through reading this book.

—Robby Richardson
Executive Director, Internet Evangelism Network
Billy Graham Center (Wheaton, IL)

Chapter One

Casting an Electronic Net

I am in the habit of staying up late at night, talking to friends on instant messenger, and checking e-mail."

Kristi is one of the 1.7 billion people in the world who currently use the Internet on a regular basis.[1] Like millions of young people, she uses the Web not only for information but primarily as a way of staying in touch with her friends.

When Kristi first encountered God on the Web, she was a smart, successful young lady, beginning her college career at the prestigious University of Virginia. She loved to chat with friends on the Internet—and she had little time for church or Christianity.

"I didn't think that organized religion was an important thing. It wasn't necessary and I had no interest whatsoever."

Like so many others, Kristi had been disappointed by overzealous believers in the past. "I had some bad experiences with people saying, 'Oh, you're going to hell.' I would have been very turned off if someone would have come up and tried to evangelize me on the street."

But despite her suspicions of organized religion, she did have questions about God and the meaning of life. "I was too scared to find someone at a church to ask questions."

Kristi was lost, yet she sailed through her existence, ignoring the nagging questions within. That is, until she began seeing "the T-shirt message"—an ad for an Internet evangelism site promoted by young believers on college campuses.

"I went to visit James Madison University where my best friend was attending. When I was there, I saw a lot of EveryStudent.com posters in dorm room windows and on dorm-room doors. I had seen the EveryStudent address many times. My friend, Adam, actually had an EveryStudent.com T-shirt that he would wear.

"So I just decided, 'Why not—I might as well go to this site.' I read one article after another. I have no clue how much time I spent the first time I was on the site—an hour or more."

Kristi read about issues relevant to her life and concepts she struggled to understand. Her heart was touched. "It really spoke to me as a seeker, someone who was searching. It was directive, right where I was. And it answered very real issues—things that had been troubling me."

Like so many young people, Kristi was asking the big questions:

- "How can there be only one truth?"
- "How does religion and Christianity impact my life?"
- "Is there hope for a lasting marriage?"

"I also went to some of the articles that were more intellectual, discussing the differences between other world religions, and why I should choose the God of the Bible."

Then she found the prayer to invite Jesus into her heart.

Up to that point, Kristi had never known that a person could pray such a prayer. "It was something I had never thought about, that God could be living within me. I was blown away that I could actually have a relationship with God."

And so, sitting by herself in her dorm room, staring at a Web site on her computer, Kristi invited Jesus Christ to be her Lord and Savior.

"I remember sitting there in my pajamas at my desk chair, just praying and crying. I was so happy."

A Virtual Tidal Wave

Today millions of people like Kristi are active Internet users around the world. Remarkably it is now possible for any Bible-believing Christian to potentially reach one-fourth of the world's population from their dining room table.[2] And someone with a mobile phone, PDA, or another portable digital device is now linked electronically to half of the people living on planet Earth.

The world is connected like never before.

The Internet is a new and dynamic tool for bringing the Good News to the masses. The world is now meeting and talking on the World Wide Web—and so the potential to share the gospel of Jesus Christ with seekers like Kristi is enormous.

Some of the recent breakthroughs in the Internet and digital technology paint an exciting picture:

- Microsoft and other leading computer experts have called the social network explosion the second phase of the Internet's development—or Web 2.0.
- According to Alexa Web Search, Facebook, YouTube, Blogger, MySpace, Twitter, and WordPress—some of the leading social networks in the world—are among the top twenty most-viewed Web sites.[3] They are now more popular than eBay, Amazon, AOL, and Hotmail.
- According to Reuters, approximately 80 percent of the U.S. population is online.[4]
- According to a May 2009 report by The Radicati Group, there were 1.4 billion e-mail users in 2009. That number is expected to rise to 1.9 billion by 2013. The same study found that approximately 247 billion e-mails are sent each day.[5]
- Nearly 100 percent of college graduates are online and 90 percent use e-mail daily, according to a study conducted by

the Pew organization.[6]

- More than 81 percent of teens are online (Pew).[7]

We are witnessing an explosion of social networks online—Web sites that allow people to post a Web page for free (or for a minimal cost) and connect with people around the world.

- Facebook is the fastest-growing Web site in the world according to the Web traffic tracking site hitgeist.com.[8]
- News Corp., the giant media company owned by Rupert Murdoch, acquired MySpace in the fall of 2005 for $580 million. Industry experts say MySpace was worth $6.5 billion in 2009. Facebook was valued at $10 billion at the same time.[9]

J. C. R. Licklider, one of the pioneers of the Internet, peered into the future in 1960 and made this remarkable prophetic observation: "In due course [the computer] will be part of the formulation of problems: part of real-time thinking, problem-solving, doing of research, conducting of experiments, getting into the literature and finding references."

While this first part of Licklider's quote predicted the initial stage of Internet growth, the second part predicted what has come to be known as Web 2.0: "And it will mediate and facilitate communication among human beings."[10] His amazing prediction is coming true today in ways that Licklider likely never dreamed possible, drawing the world together into one electronic global community.

Into God

This new connectivity could not have come at a more strategic moment in history. Around the world people are moving from the countryside into the wired megacities—and they are hungry for God like never before. The terms *God* and *religion* continue to rank in the top five Web searches (sex and pornography topics are usually number one).

People like Kristi are eagerly logging on to find answers to their questions about God, religion, and spirituality.

- According to Pew, 64 percent of Americans are seeking spiritual information on the Internet.[11]
- George Barna believes that currently fifty million people may rely on the Internet to provide their faith-based experiences.[12]
- Heidi Campbell, a Texas A&M professor who studies religion on the Internet, said, "Almost two-thirds of people that go online at some point have done so . . . to seek out religious information, or to get involved in a religious conversation or for other [religious] purposes."[13]

There have never been more people yearning for spiritual truth in the history of the world. The time is ripe for Bible-believing Christians to go online with a compelling, professional presentation that greets these seekers with biblical truth.

The gospel message never changes—our presentation of it must evolve and adapt constantly to the ever-changing culture.

Spirituality is in—but not necessarily Christianity. In this postmodern era, it's cool to be a seeker, but the exclusivity of following Jesus Christ, "the way, the truth and the life," is more difficult for postmodern thinkers.

As this new era dawns, people are flocking to the Internet to learn about spirituality. Reggie McNeal wrote in *The Present Future*, "Although intrigue with institutional religion is down, interest in spirituality is up. A 2003 Gallup poll indicates that a vast majority of Americans say that religion has an impact on every area of their life."[14]

What's Up Ahead?

In his book *The Road Ahead*, Bill Gates, founder and chairman of Microsoft, explained, "We are watching something historic happen, and it will affect the world seismically." Gates said that he was "thrilled" to be able to squint "into the future and [catch] that first revealing hint of revolutionary possibilities" at this "beginning of an epochal change," the most massive economic shift since the Industrial Revolution.[15]

I found an interesting quote regarding change in the world of communication:

> An incredible new technology enables the transmission of text on a worldwide basis. It rapidly reduces production and distribution costs and for the first time allows large numbers of people to access text and pictures in their own homes.[16]

You might suppose this quote referred to the Internet, but you would be wrong. It's describing the Gutenberg printing press—an invention that revolutionized the world and led to the Reformation in the church and the Enlightenment in the secular world.

Using the latest technology to spread the gospel has been part of God's evangelism strategy for the church since the beginning. Paul gave us insight into this concept when he wrote to the Corinthian church:

> For although I am free from all people, I have made myself a slave to all, in order to win more people. To the Jews I became like a Jew, to win Jews; to those under the law, like one under the law—though I myself am not under the law—to win those under the law. To those who are outside the law, like one outside the law—not being outside God's law, but under the law of Christ—to win those outside the law. To the weak I became weak, in order to win the weak. I have become all things to all people, so that I may by all means save some. (1 Cor. 9:19–22)

The Internet has become a twenty-first-century Roman road. But it is also a worldwide marketplace, a theater, front porch and backyard fence, and an office watercooler. The World Wide Web can be like an electronic train terminal connecting all the various parts of your evangelism strategy and providing the crucial means for people to respond directly to the gospel message.

Digital devices and the Internet represent a convergence of media in one delivery mechanism—including video, print, telephone, video games, e-mail, social networks, blogs, online television, audio and video phone—the list goes on and on. As a result, Internet evangelists are putting these tools to use while harnessing the energy of exploding social networks to connect with searching souls all over the world.

Waking the Fishermen

But the church has yet to fully embrace this Internet revolution—especially regarding evangelism on the Web. Leonard Sweet expressed his frustration with the church's apparent technophobia:

> At a time when science and technology are having an adrenaline rush, few in the church get IT (with IT referring to Information Technology). The notoriously technophobic mainline (then old line) church has drifted beyond the "sidelines."[17]

But there is a stirring taking place among the NetCasters who sense that the Internet waters are rolling with fish. The fishers of men are beginning to recognize the immense potential for harvest that exists through the World Wide Web. They are mending their nets, fitting out their vessels, and sending out the call for NetCasters to rise up and seize this glorious day for the fulfillment of the Great Commission.

A Safe Place to Go

Our friend Kristi from the University of Virginia says the Internet provided the comfortable environment she needed to get answers to her spiritual questions.

"I don't know that I would have explored matters and issues as deeply if I hadn't had that safe place to go where I didn't feel silly asking questions and seeking out answers. It guided me to Christ and presented the gospel in such a real way.

"I continued to visit EveryStudent.com and dialogued with a few people through the Web site. I was so excited to get their responses. I was checking my e-mail several times a day because I wanted to know what these new friends had to say—I wanted these questions answered. The people who responded were so kind and joyful, and they told me they would be praying for me. I was amazed that they loved me so much through these e-mails.

"After I went to the site and I became a Christian, I wanted to share EveryStudent.com with other people; and I wanted my friends to ask about it, so I actually borrowed Adam's T-shirt and started wearing it around my school. People would stop and ask me about it.

"EveryStudent.com led me to the most important decision I have ever made and the best thing that has ever happened to me in my whole life. I didn't think that anything on the Web could actually change my life. But it did, and I now realize that was just God directing me to what would be the best way to reach me.

"That was God—using this tool that I was on every single day—to reach me."

There are millions of people like Kristi, searching for God, seeking truth and answers on the Internet. And Jesus commands us to go and meet them where they are—taking a never-changing message into an ever-changing world.

It is clear that on the one hand, traditional church membership is in sharp decline, and on the other hand, the adoption of communication through the Internet and Web-based communication is rapidly growing around the world. I believe the time has come for the church to adopt an Internet evangelism strategy, train individual saints in online outreach and encourage creative Internet ministry, and harness the tremendous power of the Internet to take the gospel to this burgeoning online population.

It is time for the NetCasters to arise!

Like the man from Macedonia in the apostle Paul's vision (see Acts 16:9–10), the sea of humanity is calling to you, "Come online and help us." Jesus said He would make us fishers of men. Are you ready to become a NetCaster?

Chapter Two

Fishers of Men:
Why Cast Our Nets?

Kathi was a witch—a dedicated Wiccan who had a "family" of gods she served, and whom she thought served her. But after receiving two visions of Jesus calling her to Himself, she put God to a test. As the Lord would have it, a NetCaster named Rich Tatum was part of God's answer to her call.

While working at *Christianity Today* as a Web project manager, Rich was about to leave the office one day at about 5:30 p.m. when he was pulled into this relationship. To aid in keeping up with issues surrounding his job, Rich was a member of a few newsletter discussion lists. Every day, questions landed in his inbox from fellow technicians needing help. Rich and others would ask and answer questions as they could.

"It had been several weeks since I'd culled through the messages from this discussion group," Rich remembers. That night he suddenly felt an urge to check his mail folder. "I didn't have anything pressing going on, and it would be one less thing to do in the morning. But, 'Nah,' I thought. 'Just leave it.'"

Rich got up to go home, but he couldn't bring himself to leave. As he headed for the door, he felt the compulsion again. "Just check the folder."

Sighing, he sat back down and worked as quickly as he could. About half an hour later, he had winnowed several hundred messages down to three that needed attention. "A couple of e-mails were informational pieces I could use, but one was a plea for help. It was from Kathi Sharpe, and her question was probably two or three months old by now. But, still, nobody had answered her.

"I thought to myself that I'd take care of it the next day. I'd want to take my time with it, provide screenshots and supporting material. It could take some time."

So he closed his mail and got up to leave. But he was stopped again. "Answer it."

"What?" he questioned. "It's 6:00. The answer will take me at least another hour or two to prepare. She's waited three months; another day won't hurt."

Still he kept thinking, *Answer it!*

Sighing again, Rich sat back down and banged out as thorough an answer that a quick reply would allow. He copied Kathi's e-mail directly, to make sure she saw his answer. And, as predicted, it was at least another couple hours before he could head out the door. But this time he felt no compulsion to stay.

The next morning Rich received an e-mail from Kathi that blew his mind. "My note, apparently, was a direct answer to prayer. And what followed in instant messages over the course of the next year or so was a conversion story and discipling process that taught me more about faith and God's faithfulness than I could have ever imagined."

What Rich didn't know was that Kathi was a practicing pagan witch, a Wiccan. God had been working on her heart, leading her to Himself, entering into her dreams, and answering her prayers.

The night before Rich responded to her work-related question, Kathi went to bed and prayed, setting out a "fleece," telling God that if He really wanted her to listen to Him, then He'd better have an answer to her question waiting in her inbox in the morning. Her job was on the line, and if she didn't solve this problem now, she'd be out of work.

That next morning she was stunned. Not only was her question answered and her job saved, but the e-mail came from an employee of *Christianity Today*. Furthermore, it was from someone within the Assemblies of God denomination—the only church she'd visited in recent years. "As far as prayers go, for Kathi, this was the trifecta," Rich said later, "a neat little hat trick that did more to bring her to salvation than anything anyone else had to say to her."

So since God had filled their appointment books, Kathi and Rich began chatting fairly regularly.

"I was very dedicated to what I thought were gods," Kathi explains, "with zero plans of ever changing. I had two dreams, the second of which left me shattered and having to come to some sort of conclusion about who Jesus was. If I'd tried to ignore Him, I think I might have gone mad. Yet I wasn't going to lay it all down without some sort of proof."

In July, Kathi had her first dream of Jesus.

"My reaction was dual—wonder at why He, of all possible deities, would show up in my dreams, and anger that He'd have the audacity to do so. After all, He wasn't one of my gods, and I didn't want any part of Him. I told Him to go away, to leave me be!"

The following Saturday night Kathi had another dream. In this one, Jesus appeared clearly and spoke to her in sign language—a language she had not yet learned but recognized the need to since she was losing her hearing.

When she woke up the next morning, Kathi looked up the words in a sign dictionary. Jesus had signed very clearly, "Come, follow Me."

"It couldn't get any plainer," Kathi said. "I was being called."

Their daughter attended an Assembly of God church, so Kathi and her husband went to the morning and evening services that Sunday. "I was determined, though, to not veer from my chosen path," Kathi explains. "I didn't want to give up my gods, my complacent life, and the level of comfortability."

But Kathi had many unanswered questions and felt that Christianity "in general" was responsible for most of the mess the world is in today.

"I spent both services in tears, torn between what I knew must be, and what I thought I wanted. I also spent some time talking to Christian friends, people who knew my history and knew what making a decision to follow Jesus would mean to me."

She couldn't figure out how she could give up paganism to follow Jesus. "My whole identity was focused on being pagan. I was a leader in the community online. I was respected as being a powerful witch. And my gods were family. But I could not refuse the call of Jesus."

By Monday Kathi was coming close to surrendering to Jesus, but she wanted some proof. "Dreams can come from anywhere. So Monday night I prayed for the problems I'd been having with a piece of software I'm responsible for at work to be resolved. This issue had been giving me gray hair for some time, and in spite of asking for help of other people who use this software (weeks before), I'd gotten none. Tuesday afternoon, in my mail, was a letter from Rich Tatum, telling me how to resolve my problem.

"Now, imagine me, a pagan still in heart, having prayed to a God that I didn't really believe in, and then getting a nearly immediate answer from somebody from *Christianity Today* online!

"I asked God Himself to show me that He was real, and I asked Him to do so in a very specific way. He responded by sending Rich my way—first to answer that prayer in a way far more specific than I could ever have imagined, then to show me the way to Jesus."

Rich spent hours talking to Kathi online the next day. He told her, among other things, the story of Saul's conversion and answered many of her questions. At one point that day, Kathi made the decision in her heart to do as Jesus said and to follow Him. "Over the next two days, my heart became light, and I knew that I had finally come home."

Today Kathi and her husband are serving in full-time ministry, and their son is called to missions work. The whole family has come to faith. Since her dramatic conversion, Kathi has gained a lot of experience with

Internet evangelism. The staff at ExWitch.org successfully used one of Kathi's message boards for six years for that purpose.

Kathi explains how Internet evangelism played a key role in her coming to Christ out of paganism. "Recognize that having an online component, especially for people with unique backgrounds, such as leaving the occult, can fill in gaps that local churches are hard-pressed to provide."

"I don't think that Internet evangelism should ever replace face-to-face witnessing," says Kathi. "Jesus said for us to go and make disciples, and we should use every opportunity to do so, anytime someone's available to talk to. Maybe if we start looking at all our interactions with other people as 'divine opportunities,' more people would come to know Jesus."

Taking the Word to the World

Just as Rich brought the Word of God to Kathi and now Kathi is taking the gospel to others, Jesus has called each one of us to be fishers of men, being obedient to Christ's Great Commission:

> "Go, therefore, and make disciples of all nations, baptizing them in the name of the Father and of the Son and of the Holy Spirit, teaching them to observe everything I have commanded you. And remember, I am with you always, to the end of the age." (Matt. 28:19–20)

This is the calling of every Bible-believing Christian. But it's important to understand that what Jesus was saying to His disciples here—and to us—was not some new plan of God's. From the beginning of creation, His intention was that His people would be His caretakers, bringing His message of love to the nations.

The arrival of Jesus Christ—the Word made flesh—is the culmination of God's missionary purpose to redeem mankind to Himself. This missionary purpose, the sending of the Word to the world, began with creation—and more specifically, the creation of man in the Garden of Eden.

> Then God said, "Let Us make man in Our image, according to Our likeness. They will rule the fish of the sea, the birds of the sky, the animals, all the earth, and the creatures that crawl on the earth." (Gen. 1:26)

God gave dominion to man and made him His regent or ambassador on the earth to oversee His creation for Him. God gave man responsibility in the world—dominion or authority—to tend it, name the animals, and carry out His will on this planet.

The Word through Israel

It's important to understand that God was making a dramatic gesture in coming into a covenantal relationship with man once again through Abraham. When Adam and Eve disobeyed His word to them, man's relationship with God was broken. The original Edenic Covenant, granting mankind dominion, was still in place; but God's plan for man to rightly rule on the earth through a loving relationship with Him was blocked by sin. Though God had relationship with man through people like Abel, Seth, Enoch, and Noah, the vast majority of mankind had rejected God.

Through the covenants with Abraham, Isaac, and Jacob, God was reestablishing a personal, loving relationship with man.

> "As for Me, My covenant is with you, and you will become the father of many nations." (Gen. 17:4)

God blessed Abraham with the son of promise, Isaac. But then God tested Abraham, calling on him to offer up Isaac. When Abraham obeyed, placing Isaac on the altar, raising the knife, and then plunging it downward, the angel of the Lord stopped his hand. Then the voice of the Lord spoke to Abraham:

> "And all the nations of the earth will be blessed by your offspring because you have obeyed My command." (Gen. 22:18)

Abraham was the father of many nations as God promised, both through natural Israel by blood and spiritual Israel by faith. So it is through the sacrifice of Jesus, the seed, that God's promise is fulfilled, that "all the nations of the earth will be blessed by your offspring" (22:18).

John Stott says of the Abrahamic Covenant, "God made a promise . . . to Abraham. And an understanding of that promise is indispensable to an understanding of the Bible and of the Christian mission. These are perhaps the most unifying verses in the Bible; the whole of God's purpose is encapsulated here."[1]

God made the same covenant promise to Isaac: "I will make your offspring as numerous as the stars of the sky, I will give your offspring all these lands, and all the nations of the earth will be blessed by your offspring" (Gen. 26:4).

Then God made the same covenant promise to Jacob: "Your offspring will be like the dust of the earth, and you will spread out toward the west, the east, the north, and the south. All the peoples on earth will be blessed through you and your offspring" (Gen. 28:14).

So the call of God through Abraham, Isaac, Jacob, and their descendents, the chosen people, Israel, was always to take the Word to the world. Through Israel—both natural and spiritual—all the families of the earth were to be blessed.

The Word to the World through Jesus

In His earthly ministry, Jesus affirmed this missionary purpose of God. Through His love and compassion, Jesus demonstrated the love of Abba for the entire world to see. Jesus picked up the missionary calling after the nation of Israel failed to fulfill it.

John Stott writes, "Although Israel is described as 'a light to lighten the nations,' and has a mission to bring forth justice to the nations" (see Isa. 42:1–4, 6; 49:6), we do not actually see this happening. It is only in the Lord Jesus himself that these prophecies are fulfilled, for only in his day are the nations actually included in the redeemed community."[2]

Because Jesus is the head, and we are the body, the ministry of Jesus in the earth has been extended to us. We see a key example as Jesus activated His disciples to be His witnesses. In verse 1 of Luke 10, Jesus sent out the seventy to take the gospel to Israel.

> After this, the Lord appointed 70 others, and He *sent them* ahead of Him in pairs to every town and place where He Himself was about to go. (Luke 10:1, emphasis added)

The Greek word in verse 1 is *apostello*, which means literally "to send." But then in verse 2, Jesus amplified the meaning behind what He was doing.

> He told them: "The harvest is abundant, but the workers are few. Therefore, pray to the Lord of the harvest to *send out* workers into His harvest." (Luke 10:2, emphasis added)

The Greek in this verse behind the English phrase "send out" is *ekballo*, which means "to expel, to drive out, cast out, or thrust out."

Gordon Robertson explains, "When Jesus would drive out a demon, He would *ekballo* it. When Jesus drove the money changers from the temple with a whip of cords, the Greek is *ekballo*. Translating *ekballo* as a gentle "send out" doesn't do the word justice."[3]

In sending out the seventy and in encouraging them to pray that the Lord of the harvest would *ekballo* the disciples, Jesus was demonstrating the heart and purpose of God to thrust out laborers to reap the harvest. Here is the fulfillment of the protoevangel of Genesis 3:15—both through Jesus, and through us!

It is significant that when the seventy returned, rejoicing that demons were subject to them, Jesus nearly quoted verbatim God's promise to Adam and Eve in Genesis 3:

> The Seventy returned with joy, saying, "Lord, even the demons submit to us in Your name."

> He said to them, "I watched Satan fall from heaven
> like a lightning flash. Look, I have given you the
> *authority to trample on snakes* and scorpions and over all
> the power of the enemy; nothing will ever harm you."
> (Luke 10:17–19, emphasis added)

Jesus extended both His authority and His missionary calling to the disciples—not only those seventy, but all of His disciples, at all times, in all places. Christians have been adopted into the family of God through faith in the atoning work of Jesus Christ.

The apostle Paul confirmed this sonship and this calling by declaring:

> The Spirit Himself testifies together with our spirit
> that we are God's children, and if children, also
> heirs—*heirs of God and co-heirs with Christ*—seeing that
> we suffer with Him so that we may also be glorified
> with Him. (Rom. 8:16–17, emphasis added)

Paul also confirmed the believer's inclusion in the missionary call of God to destroy the works of the Devil when he wrote:

> The God of peace will soon crush Satan *under your feet*.
> The grace of our Lord Jesus be with you. (Rom. 16:20,
> emphasis added)

God's plan is for believers to join in the missional calling of Genesis 3:15, working in conjunction with Jesus to crush the head of the Serpent and bring the kingdom of God to Earth:

> The Son of God was revealed for this purpose: to
> destroy the Devil's work. (1 John 3:8)

Before He ascended into heaven, Jesus told His disciples that the Holy Spirit would be given to empower the church to carry out God's plan to take the Word to the world. In these final instructions to His disciples, Jesus once again reaffirmed the purpose of God through the church:

"But you will receive power when the Holy Spirit
has come upon you, and *you will be My witnesses* in
Jerusalem, in all Judea and Samaria, and to the ends of
the earth." (Acts 1:8, emphasis added)

So the Great Commission is, in fact, the great reminder. As spiritual
Israel, from the Day of Pentecost until the return of Jesus Christ, the
church is called to carry forth the great missionary calling of God by
making disciples of all nations (Greek: *ethnos*).

Today God has given us the Internet as an amazing tool to fulfill
this missionary calling.

Harnessing Technology to Preach the Gospel

But this is nothing new. At each major phase in the development of
the church, the Holy Spirit inspired believers to use the latest developments
in travel and communication to carry out the Great Commission. Many
believe these new innovations—the Greek language, Roman roads, sail-
ing ships, the Gutenberg printing press, locomotives, automobiles, radio,
airplanes, television, and satellite communications—were providentially
supplied by God to carry the gospel from one generation to the next.

During the Renaissance, Europeans suddenly gained a new appre-
ciation for science, art, and literature. It was an era marked by a rejec-
tion of superstition and unchecked religious dogma. In Germany,
Britain, and France there was a renewed interest in the systematic study
of Scripture, with an emphasis on the examination of the Greek and
Hebrew texts of the Bible.

This revival of scholarship helped ignite the flames of the Protestant
Reformation, and the bold teachings of Luther, Calvin, and others.

From the advent of the written page, books had been distributed
only as quickly as they could be hand-copied. Prior to Gutenberg's press,
it cost a working man a year's wages to purchase a Bible. The church
harnessed the technology of the day, the invention of the printing press
by Johannes Gutenberg in 1456, and the Holy Spirit used it to carry the
Reformers' message to all of Europe and beyond.

The burgeoning desire of the time was to know God's Word, and it's significant that the first book printed by Gutenberg was the Bible. The printing press brought the Scriptures into common use as Luther and other Reformers translated and circulated the Bible into many of the languages of Europe. The people, both common and noble, who read the Bible soon realized that the Roman Catholic Church of the time was far removed from the New Testament ideal. Soon books and pamphlets written by the Reformers were being read throughout Europe and beyond.

In the centuries preceding the Reformation, both John Wycliffe and John Huss preached the same basic message as Luther's, but they were not successful in igniting the fires of Reformation. According to church tradition, as Huss was being burned at the stake for his biblical teachings, he prophesied this explosion of God's missional purpose on the earth.

> You are now roasting the goose, [*huss* means "goose" in Bohemian] but in a hundred years there will rise up a swan that you shall not roast nor scorch. Him men will hear sing and God will allow him to live.[4]

It was only after the invention of the printing press—a key communication technology that helped usher in the Reformation, Renaissance, and Enlightenment—that both the Bible and the teachings of Luther and the other Reformers were distributed far and wide in books, pamphlets, and leaflets. As the people received the truth of God's Word in their own language, their eyes became enlightened to God's will and change came in their hearts and minds.

Modern Marvels and Gospel Pioneers

In the early part of the twentieth century, Christian evangelists and missionaries seized the modern invention of radio to take the Word to the world. Another technological tool used effectively by evangelists in the twentieth century was motion pictures. Ministries like the Billy Graham Evangelistic Association, with its World Wide Pictures film production arm, and Campus Crusade for Christ, with *The Jesus Film*, have used movies to take the gospel to millions around the world. Campus Crusade has used *The Jesus Film* so effectively that it is now the most-watched film in the history of the world.[5] Since its creation, *The Jesus Film* has been translated into 810 languages and has been seen by more than 3.5 billion people."[6]

In the 1950s ministers like Oral Roberts, Archbishop Fulton Sheen, and Rex Humbard harnessed the technology of television to preach the gospel to the world.

"The vast majority of people do not go to church and the only way we can reach them is through TV," Humbard said in his autobiographical book *Miracles in My Life*. "We must go into their homes— into their hearts—to bring them the gospel of Jesus Christ." By 1970 Humbard's syndicated program appeared on more TV stations in America than any other television show and eventually reached more than six hundred stations.[7]

While Humbard, Roberts, and Graham developed radio and television programs, Pat Robertson, Paul Crouch, Jim Bakker, and later Morris Cerullo launched vast satellite television networks to take the Word to the world.

In 1968, as the Christian Broadcasting Network (CBN) was preparing to open its newly built television studio in Portsmouth, Virginia, the Spirit of God fell on the staff during a corporate time of prayer. "I want you to pray for the world," the Holy Spirit spoke to the heart of Pat Robertson, who wrote about the experience in his book *Shout It From the Housetops*.

> Instantly, as if He had reached His hand into my heart and enlarged it, I felt the capacity to accommodate a vision far greater than I had ever had before. . . . "I want you to claim the world for Jesus," the Holy Spirit was directing. I heard myself praying with great power, and felt an enormous faith building in my heart that the entire world could, indeed, hear the good news of Jesus. It was not an impossible task—just a

difficult one—and God was calling me to help bring it to pass.[8]

Today CBN's programs can be seen in more than 160 nations of the world. As the new millennium dawned, CBN had expanded its television outreach to the point that more programming was done in the indigenous language and culture of nations outside the United States than inside. The ministries of the Trinity Broadcasting Network and the PTL Television Network, which became the INSP Network, followed CBN's lead.

God's Missional Mandate Today

These twentieth-century pioneers harnessed the communication, technological, and travel advances of their day to take the Word to the world. Now, with the dawn of the new millennium, unprecedented opportunities abound through the Internet and digital technology to share the gospel of Jesus Christ in creative and influential ways.

Allan Beeber of Campus Crusade's Global Media Outreach—a ministry that has led more than a million people to the Lord through the Internet—sees unlimited potential through digital technology. "Through the use of CDs, DVDs, and streaming media, the evangelism world is offering a host of new options. The issue is to get the message out in a form that seekers are currently accessing."[9]

Dr. Sterling Huston, chairman of the Internet Evangelism Network Executive Committee, declares, "We need to put the gospel in a language and format that communicates with new generations; in a way so that they respond, in Internet-relevant presentations."[10]

"The truth of the gospel never changes, but the methods of delivering the truth must change to meet our culture. We have a great opportunity, particularly with children and with young adults. The National Center for Education says 90 percent of U.S. children and adolescents ages five through 17 have access to a computer and use one. Sixty percent are online. And among those 15 to 17, 75 percent of them are online. Among college students, 98 percent have access to the Net. This is where we will find them. This is where we need to meet them."[11]

Today NetCasters are taking up the torch and carrying this gospel message to the World through the World Wide Web. You can be a part of this NetCasters' revolution. Read on to find out how!

Chapter Three

Weaving the Nets: Building Your Internet Presence

The *Time* magazine 2006 Person of the Year was you—the individual. The Internet made this possible.

In declaring every person the Person of the Year in 2006, *Time* was recognizing a basic, fundamental shift in the state of communication, information, and ideas in this new millennium—and this was all made possible by the advent of the Internet—and more recently Web 2.0.

The editors of *Time* said this to justify their controversial selection of the 2006 Person of the Year:

> Look at 2006 through a different lens and you'll see another story, one that isn't about conflict or great men. It's a story about community and collaboration on a scale never seen before. . . . It's about the many wresting power from the few and helping one another for nothing and how that will not only change the world, but also change the way the world changes.

The new Web is a very different thing. It's a tool for bringing together the small contributions of millions of people and making them matter. Silicon Valley consultants call it Web 2.0, as if it were a new version of some old software. But it's really a revolution.[1]

Today the Internet is about relationships and communication—information, while still important, is secondary.

Definition of Internet Evangelism

To understand effective Internet evangelism, we first need to define what it is. Tony Whittaker is a leading NetCaster based in the United Kingdom who edits the monthly Web Evangelism Bulletin. He is also the driving force behind the annual Internet Evangelism Day, cosponsored by the U.S.-based Internet Evangelism Network (IEN). I asked him to describe what he believes to be effective outreach on the Web.

"Effective Internet evangelism almost always is one-on-one because a person reading a page is, of course, always one person. And so a writer should always be writing as if to one person, not preaching as if to a congregation. The gifts needed for a Web writer are those of a journalist, not a preacher. A preacher has a captive audience who has already decided to attend church, or another church-like event. A Web writer has no captive audience, since they can click away within seconds if they do not like the page. He or she must know how to write enticingly and keep the reader going down the page.

"Any conception of Web evangelism as some sort of magical broadcast effect that reaches people automatically is, of course, misplaced, just as TV broadcasting does not either. People actually have to decide to tune in for TV or click on a link, for the Web, and then decide to stick around.

"This concern about 'real' evangelism only being face-to-face evangelism is certainly something I come across. I guess some answers to this concern would be that most actual conversions I ever read about online usually result from a considerable time of e-mail (or similar) discussion and mentoring. Although I am sure it happens that people read something and come to faith immediately, just as they may when receiving a tract or watching something on TV, in practice these things are only one link in a chain, and ongoing contact with a real, praying, person is actually the way it happens most of the time, just as in the non-Web world."

Web evangelists, or NetCasters, have found ways in which an Internet-based relationship is both different and less deep than a face-to-face relationship. There is, on the other side, that sense of being able to ask and discuss with someone online things you would perhaps find hard or impossible to talk through face-to-face.

"For many people, face-to-face evangelism is not an option," Whittaker explains. "Only if every person in the world had a good relationship with someone they knew as a Christian, or were likely to frequently meet a known Christian in a setting where they could share their faith, would other methods of evangelism not be needed. In many countries, the chances of ever meeting an evangelical are slim—Eastern Europe, Japan, or the Middle East, for example. Therefore Web evangelism becomes even more strategic in these places."

The 99 to 1 Problem

Millions of Christians around the world are now on the Internet every day. As I have pointed out, globally, approximately 1.7 billion people are logging onto the Web on an ongoing basis.[2] The world is flocking to the Internet and digital media outlets. The Web is now the new electronic meeting place, especially for people age thirty and under.

The problem is that, just as in the real world, Christians and non-Christians are barely talking to each other online. While it seems that everyone is on the Web, there is a major disconnect between the majority of Bible-believing Christians and the rest of the online subculture.

Tony Whittaker has named this phenomenon the "99 percent rule since Christian Web sites are created for other Christians, while only 1 percent of Christian Web sites are designed to evangelize the lost.[3]

We can see this same rule reflected in Christian book and music publishing as well; an examination of titles and videos reveals that the vast majority of material, in terms of language, content, and worldview, is produced entirely for Christians. The lack of truly evangelistic Web sites in the English language (let alone other languages) is a tremendous problem facing the church today. The vast majority of Web sites with Christian content are targeted to a Christian audience for the purpose of information or discipleship.

In order for the NetCaster to overcome this 99 to 1 problem, he or she must first recognize the importance of stepping out of his or her comfort zones and into something that might be new and different. And they must have a thorough understanding of what the Internet is and what methods are effective in catching the attention of the masses and directing them to Christ.

That chasm between those who need to know Jesus as their Savior and those who are actually doing Internet evangelism is very wide indeed. But people around the world are going online every day seeking truth. There is an incredible opportunity for evangelism and discipleship on the Internet.

"God is behind Internet evangelism in a very real and powerful way," says NetCaster John Edmiston. "People do their secret thinking on the Internet, and because of that people explore things on the Web—such as who Jesus Christ is—that they can't or won't explore in public."[4]

Walt Wilson, founder and chairman of Global Media Outreach, agrees that the Internet provides a golden opportunity to reach the nations for Christ. "You and I are the first generation to hold the technology to reach every person with the gospel and to accomplish the task of the Great Commission. What is our strategy to tell people about Jesus?" he challenges. "Will we act on what we believe?"[5]

In order to harness the power of the Internet for evangelism, the NetCaster must have a firm understanding of the current state of digital technology, and also a sense of where the Internet is going from here.

Internet and Modern Communication

The Internet is rapidly evolving—constantly reinventing itself. Convergence, community, collaboration, and interactivity are the words that best describe the direction the Internet is taking in this new millennium. In his groundbreaking book *Wikinomics*, futurist and Internet analyst Don Tapscott, along with Anthony D. Williams, shares the results of a $9 million research project that investigated how collaboration through Internet communities is creating an explosion in innovation, communication, creativity, and mankind's overall knowledge.

"From the Internet's inception its creators envisioned a universal substrate linking all mankind and its artifacts in a seamless, interconnected Web of knowledge," Tapscott and Williams observe. "This was the World Wide Web's great promise: an Alexandrian library of all past and present information and a platform for collaboration to unite communities of all stripes in any conceivable act of creative enterprise.

"The Internet is becoming a giant computer that everyone can program, providing a global infrastructure for creativity, participation, sharing, and self-organization. . . . The new Web is fundamentally different in both its architecture and applications. . . . Whether people are creating, sharing, or socializing, the new Web is principally about participating rather than about passively receiving information.

"The bottom line is this: The immutable, standalone Web site is dead. Say hello to a Web that increasingly looks like a library full of chatty components that interact and talk to one another. . . . This makes it very easy to build new Web services out of the existing components by mashing them together in fresh combinations."[6]

This "new Web" that Tapscott and Williams describe has come to be known as Web 2.0. The thrilling news for the NetCaster is that most people who receive Christ online come to the point of praying a prayer of salvation through one-on-one relationships that are built naturally. These kinds of personal relationships and conversations have exploded in growth through the advent of Web 2.0—and all the interactivity it encourages.

The Emergence of Web 2.0

Web 2.0 represents the convergence of a number of elements that make up the modern Internet: broadband penetration, online video, and communication tools like e-mail, chat, forums and message boards, individualized content creation, social networking, microblogs, blogs, vlogs, mobile digital devices, and podcasting. This phenomenon presents a plethora of opportunities for the Internet evangelist to connect with seekers and point them to Jesus.

Web 2.0 can also be applied to changes in the ways software developers and end users view the Web. According to Tim O'Reilly, "Chief among those rules is this: Build applications that harness network effects to get better the more people use them. This is what I've elsewhere called 'harnessing collective intelligence.'"[7]

Author Rex Miller thinks tools like these present ministries with a huge opportunity for reaching the next generation. "Web 2.0 represents a new revolution on the Internet—open participation," he says. "It also provides a wonderful model for change and creates a critical mass that I hope unleashes an iGeneration revolution."[8]

Kevin Hendricks wrote of the phenomenon, "The simplest way to understand Web 2.0 is that it has given power to the people. While Web 1.0 was all about passive surfing, Web 2.0 is about letting everyone contribute—whether that contribution is written opinion (blogs), feedback (comments), video (YouTube), photos (Flickr), connection and community building (MySpace/Facebook/LinkedIn), or knowledge (Wikipedia).

"More than technology or community, Web 2.0 is about a new frame of mind," Hendrick's explains. "Less is more; design matters; it's OK to start small; mistakes happen; do it cheap; anyone can do it; and share. Web 2.0 is about decentralizing power and information and putting it in the hands of amateurs. And it's OK if they get something wrong or it's not as good as professionals would do it, simply because the sheer volume of information available makes up for a few deficiencies."[9]

Web 2.0 and NetCasting

Evangelism on the Web occurs as a result of relationships, and relationships online happen in large measure as a result of Web 2.0—this second generation of Web-based communities and hosted services, including social networking sites, and wikis (collaborative information sharing sites) that are intended to allow collaboration, syndication, communication, and sharing between users.[10]

So what does the emergence of these global online conversations mean for evangelism on the Web? In a word: everything.

Jesse Carey, managing editor of RelevantMagazine.com, explains the importance of Web 2.0 in building relationships online and how someone can take these concepts and incorporate them into a strategy for Web evangelism. "We always want the readers to engage with the content. With some traditional forms of media, whether it's print, radio, or television, it's on the terms of the media outlet. You have to tune in at a certain time. You have to have the right channel. You have to subscribe to the magazine. It's all on the outlet's terms. The Web 2.0 thing started with putting media in the user's terms. They can take the podcast with them wherever they go. It's the same with Web sites.

"The outgrowth is people taking ownership of the content. And that's when you start seeing user submitted content and people being able to interact with it. So in terms of using that for evangelism, on a basic level, it enables users to comment and contact other users, or to contact the author with more questions. And if that's not practical, if there are too many users, have a comment area where they can have a small community forum to discuss the ideas. If they have questions, or if they have comments, or ideas that they want to put into the conversation, enable that.

"That helps them, not only to engage and take ownership of the content, but from an evangelism perspective to get any answers that they're looking for and kind of dig deeper with the issues."

So in light of this Web 2.0 revolution, it's a mistake to create an evangelistic Web site with the idea that it will be merely "tracts on a screen." Such an approach is simply not in keeping with what the Internet has become. Instead, we must understand the Web's nature as a communication medium, recognizing that people viewing the information placed on the Internet—whether it be text, audio, video, graphics, or photos—beg to have conversations about it.

Once we see the Internet as a modern-day forum for ideas and relationships, then we must learn how to work with its inherent strengths and either avoid or understand and use its weaknesses. When we do this, we will begin to harness and use the staggering opportunities that await the NetCaster online.

Interactive and Two-way

Tony Whittaker explains that one of the greatest attractions of Web 2.0 is this interactivity. "The user controls completely what Web pages appear on his or her monitor. Each person will have a unique route of personal choice through any Web site, and across billions of Web pages around the world. The two-way nature of the Web means that the user is no longer a passive recipient. When you listen to radio, the experience is one-way—unless you can phone in or write a letter. But the Web makes it easy for users to express opinions and interact with Webmasters by e-mail or instant messenger, and discuss a site with other users by bulletin board, blog response form, or chat room. At last, "my opinion counts."

"People want to be players, not just spectators, part of the action, not on the sidelines," writes Charles Leadbeater in his book *We-Think*.[11] Just as a newspaper aims to build loyalty among its readers, a Web site can generate a sense of community—the feeling that users can identify with the site. Successful sites understand how to create welcoming interactivity.

Relationship and connection are at the heart of the Internet—and of Internet evangelism. "Before the Web, a person's circle of relationships was usually initiated by face-to-face contact, and then sustained by personal meetings, letters, or phone," Tony Whittaker explains. "Naturally, there tended to be a geographic limitation to a circle of relationships. But with the Web, relationships can be initiated and maintained online, and physical location is no longer an issue. Using the Web, people can also maintain, at least at a limited level, a much wider range of relationships.

"Relationships are, of course, a key to evangelism. Very few people become Christians merely by hearing or reading a proclamation of the gospel. Analyze a range of testimonies, including Web-mediated stories, and in almost every case, you find that an ongoing relationship with a praying Christian played a key role.

"So effective online evangelism needs to be relational."[12]

Johnnie Gnanamanickam is the Manager of Internet Development in the Digital Media Department at the Christian Broadcasting Network. Commenting on the monumental changes occurring on the Internet today as a result of the Web 2.0 revolution, he observes, "I think God had this planned all the way—because if you look at what's happening on the Internet with Web 2.0 and social networking, basically, it now becomes possible to replicate kingdom work on the Internet. We used to have it where we could push content to people on the Internet, which was great. You were preaching a message and getting it out there. But when you get to discipleship, it has to be relationships. It has to be two-way communication. You cannot have a one-way communication going on to make disciples.

"You cannot have a machine relating to someone and making a disciple. You have to have relationships built over time. Web 2.0 and social networking make that possible. You have the opportunity now to actually build a church on the Internet because these are real people talking to one another," Gnanamanickam explains. "You have real relationships that can be built over time and taken from one stage to another. You can actually really talk a person through to salvation."

The Web 2.0 transition from content to community is a vitally important shift for those involved in Internet evangelism, says writer and NetCaster Jim Watkins. "I think at first we were just slapping content up there without any real idea of creating community or creating relationships. With books and magazines you don't have a lot of back and forth. Now there is interaction. In my e-mail newsletter I'm trying to build up that relationship. So I think it's gone more from content to community."

Internet evangelists now recognize that conversations lead to relationships and relationships lead to conversions. It's no longer enough to simply post content on a Web site and hope people will find it, read it, and come to Christ. With the advent of Web 2.0, Internet evangelists are now fostering communication through rich, interactive Web sites that utilize various types of content to attract and inform the user, then encourage them to enter into conversations with other seekers, and with other believers, with the goal of praying a prayer of salvation.

The Future of the Media and Internet Evangelism

As interactivity explodes with the growth of Web 2.0 evangelistic sites, Walt Wilson of Global Media Outreach believes the need will be for shorter content online with sixty-second audio and sixty-second video cuts being the norm. While ministries should stay current on technology, Christians need to do a better job leveraging the technology that is already available because, "we haven't really even started using the full potential of the Internet for effective gospel presentation."

Wilson made the following recommendations for individuals and ministries interested in evangelism online:

- Focus on things that think, such as mobile digital devices and cell phones.
- Become an expert on search and search engines for search engine optimization.
- Become familiar with convergence among different forms of technology and communication.
- Stay in the mainstream. Ministry can't lag behind technologically as it has in the past.
- Learn how to tell the story of Christ in sixty seconds.
- Become an expert in podcasting.[13]

The Internet is constantly changing, and NetCasters need to keep up with these developments if they are to be effective. If you're on a social network, what new applications are rolling out? What opportunities are there to use them to evangelize? What new technologies and software applications are around the bend that will make it possible for me to more effectively reach people with the gospel?

A review and understanding of some of these major trends can help the NetCaster anticipate and prepare for shifts in the Internet audience, and then position their ministry to take advantage of those trends. Digital media blogger Haydn Shaughnessy provides a foreshadowing of what he sees as the direction of the media and Internet in the coming years:

- personal syndication of content
- IPTV: television over Internet networks
- personal television and citizen television
- citizen media, online newspapers, and magazines from user content
- user referrals of articles from other sources
- social bookmarking to save and categorize a personal collection of bookmarks and share them with others
- corporate and political television: running a television channel is going to become a must-do for those types of organizations
- new search engines: strong on content that evolves when people codiscover and recommend audiovisual content
- live performance
- wikis: a Web site that allows users to add and edit content collectively
- games and virtuality: massively multiplayer online games
- classifieds: Craigslist has demonstrated the appeal and effectiveness of online classifieds
- online movies: both professional and amateur
- portals: a site that the owner positions as an entrance to other sites on the Internet, typically with search engines, free e-mail, chat rooms, and other services
- online magazines: CBN.com and ChristianityToday.com are examples of strong online magazines in the Christian space
- mixed media: using a print, photography, video mélange to create a new way of telling stories[12]

All of these innovations—and more—are making the Internet a very inviting place to be today. And the democratic marketplace of the Internet will determine what will be the next Facebook, MySpace, or YouTube. The wise Web evangelist will do well to stay in touch with these changing trends and design his or her outreach accordingly.

The encouragement is that Web tools are reasonably priced and access to your target market is nearly unlimited. The real question today for ministries and individual evangelists is not whether you have a Web presence, but how much of a Web presence do you need to be as effective as possible?

Building Your NetCaster Ministry

So once you know how the Internet works, you can begin to design and build your Web outreach.

"Start with what you think you want to try to accomplish and then pick the tools," Web designer and marketer Alex Demeshkin advises. "Don't start by saying, 'Everybody's doing mobile, or video, or whatever.' Don't start with technology. The Internet is just a tool. It's the basic human nature and principles of connecting with people, being relevant, knowing who you are talking to—who they are, what their background is, what their cultural frame of reference is—that is what matters. Then you use the tools to accomplish this."

When building a Web site for an existing ministry, you need to know the goal and objectives of that organization. Is it an existing brick-and-mortar church with a large congregation and you want to develop a strong Internet presence? What kind of Web outreach you build depends on your vision and available resources.

"Building an effective Web outreach is very time-intensive," Demeshkin explains. "There is a lot of trial and error. There is a lot of experimenting and saying, 'OK, this didn't work. Let's try something else.'

"But when you know what you want to do, and you say, 'This is who I am trying to reach, and this is what I'm trying to do,' then you look at bringing in a person that is familiar with that technology."

Demeshkin explains that the biggest problem in designing an effective Web site of any kind is an intersection of marketing and technology. "That is a hard combination that makes it really difficult to nail down. Sit down and put a few heads together and look at the toolbox that you have—e-mail marketing, video, mobile, Web site, flash video, cat text messaging, databases—then you pick the tools that are appropriate for what you're trying to do."

The basic technological investment a beginning Internet evangelist needs to start entirely depends on what he's trying to accomplish. Someone can set up a blog using a system such as Blogger in about a minute. Other content management system (CMS) tools can help the NetCaster build Web sites or church sites without any technical ability, though a solid understanding how Web sites work is required.

Google, Yahoo, Network Solutions, and many others, offer free Web sites. Web service providers such as 1and1.com offer a CMS design system, inexpensive domain registration, and hosting for minimal cost.

Some of the things to consider when designing your Web outreach include:

- What is God calling you to do?
- What are your resources (money, talent, technology, time, helpers/volunteers, etc.)?
- How much server space do you have—and what methods can you use with the amount of server space available to you?
- Who is your target audience? What are their cultural, religious, political, socioeconomic, age, and gender distinctives?
- How does your calling match the needs of your target audience?
- What tools/methods will work to reach your target audience online?
- What platform or platforms will you employ to cast your net?

Once you have answered these questions, you can begin to design your outreach through your Web site, Facebook, MySpace, mobile phone, YouTube, Second Life, My.CBN.com, Tangle, MyPraize, MeetFish, or whatever avenue the Lord directs you to use.

Within these various types of Web sites and digital platforms, you will need to also decide what types of content and tools you will offer, including:

- text articles
- short video clips, or clips linked from YouTube or Tangle
- chat or instant messaging
- message boards and forums
- social networking functionality—being an incarnational presence on the Web
- e-mail
- photo sharing
- blogs and vlogs (video blogs)
- news and current events
- in-depth discipleship training materials
- cultural commentary
- testimony creation and syndication
- children and adult animation
- church-related tools and functionality
- online mentoring
- classified ads
- online dating service (like eHarmony)
- Skype (Internet telephone and video)
- online radio

Or you could use the tools already available through Facebook, Second Life, MySpace, My.CBN.com, or another social networking site. These are only some of the leading tools used by NetCasters around the world. The list of possible content choices and methods for evangelism is as endless as your creativity, energy, and resources can stretch.

Some of the other practical considerations a NetCaster needs to be aware of when launching an outreach include:

- submitting yourself under the covering of a local church or mature Christian ministry;
- balancing family, work, ministry, and other commitments in life;
- counting the spiritual costs, including time in prayer, sacrifices of other things in life that you may want to do;

- developing a statement of faith and doctrine;
- assembling your prayer covering and scheduling regular times of prayer, both individually and as a team;
- learning apologetics and Web evangelism techniques and tools;
- creating an Internet evangelism strategy master plan;
- incorporating as a not-for-profit and tax-exempt ministry, or as a for-profit business entity;
- recruiting of volunteers or hiring a professional staff—including knowledge of labor laws, tax laws, and other human resource issues;
- budgetary considerations, sustainability issues, fund-raising, marketing, and promotional endeavors;
- training your fishermen—in ministry outreach, communication techniques, technological skills, financial accounting, marketing campaigns, and public relations.

In developing your ministry strategy, the wise NetCaster must also consider:

- How often will you update your site?
- Will you respond to e-mail personally?
- How will your message boards be designed and monitored?
- What Bible translations will be used and quoted from?
- How will you respond to emergency calls, instant messages, e-mails, etc.—especially if someone is threatening suicide?
- How many chat sessions will a volunteer or employee be responding to at one time?
- Since the Internet goes to the world, how will you respond to incoming messages in other languages? Or what languages will you translate your content into? Will you provide a translation tool?

Tony Whittaker has developed a self-assessment tool to help churches design their Web sites to reach out to seekers (www. internetevangelismday.com/church-site-design.php). While Whittaker encourages Christians to be sharing their faith online, he cautions against becoming too religious in design and presentation.

"Sometimes, a site is so totally, irredeemably religious in style and appearance that I think I could not begin to try to comment, and that their Webmaster would not begin to comprehend what I was saying anyway. Such sites will, perhaps, succeed in ministering to very churchy people, and so fulfill some sort of role. But, oh dear . . ."

John Edmiston is quick to remind the NetCaster that much of the world outside of the United States and Europe is not on broadband, and so Web sites aimed at these groups need to be designed with this in mind. "If you want to reach the nations outside the U.S. and the megacities of the world, the best way to do Internet ministry right now is to set up a Web page with a clickable form at the end for responses. Design it in HTML to deal with low bandwidth. Where we are right now, still the bulk of the world is on dial-up." But he points out that broadband is rapidly increasing.

The Internet represents a convergence of media in one delivery mechanism—including video, print, telephone, video games, e-mail, social networks, linear online television, audio, and video phone—the list of potential goes on and on. Internet evangelists must consider which of these tools to use, while at the same time harnessing the energy of exploding social networks to connect with searching souls all over the world.

Flipping the Switch

The future of Internet evangelism will be made possible by the building of relationships through ongoing conversations—as a result of the Web 2.0 phenomenon. This development is critical to the growth of online ministry.

Particularly in countries that have had state-controlled media monopolies, this democratic element of the Internet will be revolutionary—socially, politically, and religiously. The freedom of expression and thought made possible by the World Wide Web will give the Internet evangelist a tremendous opportunity to reach millions who were once held in ideological and religious prison. The consequences of this new freedom of thought will most likely redraw the global map, religiously speaking, in this century—and it may redraw maps in ways we cannot predict.

With the emergence of the Web 2.0 phenomenon, people around the globe are connecting online and having conversations about life and its meaning. As the scope and application of Web 2.0 tools grow, only time will tell just how far the arm of the kingdom can reach.

"There are ways of doing church that no one has thought of yet," says Pastor and NetCaster Mark Batterson of National Community Church in Washington, D.C. "That's the thing that gets us up early and keeps us up late."[15]

Wake up, fishermen; it's time to cast your nets! In the next chapter we will examine some of the more fruitful methods being used by Web evangelists to reach the lost on the Internet today.

Chapter Four

Full Sail at Sunrise: The Daily Life of a NetCaster

"If one is truly to succeed in leading a person to a specific place, one must first and foremost take care to find him where he is and begin there. . . . In order to truly help someone else, I must understand more than he—but certainly first and foremost understand what he understands. If I do not do that, then my greater understanding does not help him at all."
—Søren Kierkegaard[1]

Internet evangelism is all about helping people. It's about helping people who do not yet know the truth that God loves them and has provided a way for them to have a relationship with Him through Jesus Christ. It's about telling them that God is not mad at them—He already poured out His wrath on Jesus on the cross.

It's about telling them that they can be free in Jesus.

But as Kierkegaard explained, to help people, you have to meet them where they are. You need to understand what he or she understands and then walk with them gently and lovingly in their discovery of the truth.

The good news is that in all of this the Holy Spirit is there to help provide the words to share. And then the Holy Spirit will bring those words to life in the heart of the person on the other end of the Internet connection or mobile phone.

Certain methods used today may be helpful to beginning Web evangelists. As we examine these techniques, it's important to remember there is no single correct way to share your faith online. First, the key is to know the demographics of your audience and its needs and expectations online. Second, you must understand your own calling from the Lord. What is it that God has for you to do? Third, you must understand the technical and communication skills required for your particular outreach. And finally, what are your financial and time limitations?

Once you have answered these questions, it's time to dive in. But, first, make sure you bathe all that you do in prayer—for intercession is the superstructure that upholds any ministry. All Internet evangelism must begin, be sustained, and conclude with dependency on the Holy Spirit through prayer.

Internet Evangelism Methods and Techniques

We have established that Internet evangelism must be relational. But how are these relationships built and maintained? Some of the leading methods include:

- Web 2.0 interaction—chat, message boards, text messaging, social network functionality, Skype, etc.;
- Affinity Web sites—created around a particular theme, hobby, or shared interest;
- Magazine Web sites, featuring a variety of topics from a biblical worldview;
- Apologetics sites, defending and explaining Christianity from an intellectual and rational position;

- Video-driven Web sites, similar to YouTube and Tangle, featuring both short-form features and long-form video sermons or teaching;
- Blogs (Web logs), microblogs, and vlogs (video Web logs);
- Synergized Web sites with other media or local church outreach;
- Skype searches;
- Online radio;
- A combination of many of these methods into one evangelistic Web site or Web outreach.

"The 'conventional' outreach Web site is going to be the most obviously effective, in the sense of bringing people to Christ," Tony Whittaker observes. "Effective evangelism not only requires people to obtain more knowledge—they must also move from a position of antagonism and indifference to a more positive viewpoint. We must not use Christian language and ideas which will mean nothing to them. In fact we must assume they have zero knowledge. We must assess our message through their eyes, not ours."[2]

Whittaker cautions that it may also be inappropriate to give a heavy "preach for a decision," at this point. "People need time to progress and understand. Instant conversions are rare. A style of presentation which bases everything around 'praying the prayer' without true understanding or preparation is counter-productive."[3]

So it's important to find out what methods and techniques are connecting with people who are seeking online. The great author Ernest Hemingway once said, "Bait the hook according to what the fish likes, not what the fisherman likes." The apostle Paul taught basically the same concept as he shared his technique for reaching the lost of his day: "I have become all things to all people, so that I may by all means save some" (1 Cor. 9:22).

Certain methods of Internet evangelism, emerging in recent years, have proven to be effective in connecting with online seekers and pulling them toward a relationship with Jesus Christ. Here are some of the more fruitful methods used by Web evangelists to reach the lost on the Internet today. This is by no means an exhaustive list of methods—there are new ideas for reaching the lost through the Internet every day. But this is a good starting point to understand what other NetCasters are doing that is bearing fruit.

Conversations 1.0: E-mail and Instant Messages

In a humorous scene in the movie *You've Got Mail*, the grandfather of Tom Hanks's character is telling him how he used to correspond through letters with a girl he liked. "You know, stamps, paper, envelopes . . ." he said, only half-jokingly. "You know, I've heard of it," Hanks's character replies. The entire movie is based on a relationship that develops via e-mail after a chance encounter in a chat room.

Surveys tell us that today nearly 100 percent of college-age students use e-mail to communicate. People age thirty and under have grown up with e-mail as a part of life.

In the book *Before I Close My Eyes: True E-mail Conversations of Faith and the Meaning of Life*, Mikael Andreasen tells the story of his e-mail conversations with Stine, a seeker of truth he had met through an Internet music forum. After meeting at his small music store, Mikael and Stine began going to concerts together and exchanging, as he puts it, "a few chatty e-mails."

One night as she closed her e-mail, Stine asked Mikael, "If you could explain to me the meaning of life before I close my eyes tonight, I would be content." That comment started a string of intense e-mail exchanges about God, skepticism, science, faith, and life in general.

Here is how Mikael responded to Stine's question, and a portion of the conversation that ensued:

Mikael: The meaning of life? Hmm, to become friends with God would be my best answer, but perhaps that's too abstract.

Stine: Do you believe in God?

Mikael: Absolutely. Although, even if I didn't, I think that would probably be the best answer I could come up with.

Stine: I'm going to have to think about that . . . if you suggest that there's meaning to life, then I assume you've already found it? I think it's quite difficult to get my head around those things . . .

Mikael: Think it over. I would be curious to hear what you'd come up with. Feel free to ask me questions if there's anything you're wondering about. I am happy to talk about my faith, especially to be challenged and provoked myself.

Stine: I found it impossible to sleep last night and lay in bed thinking and thinking. At one point I was ready to jump on my bike and ride over to you, but didn't. . . . It feels strange to say this—especially in e-mail—but I have wanted to talk to you about this for some time now, I just didn't dare . . . I don't personally believe in God, but would like to find out exactly why it is that I don't. Besides, with my adherence to science there leaves no room for a personal God—if you understand what I mean. I am, however, rather intrigued by the "big" existential questions . . . and I really don't know anyone who actually believes in God. . . . I don't want to inflict my problems on you so they become a burden, but it is nice to be able to write to someone.

Mikael took this opportunity to open up to Stine about his faith, but he made it clear he was not trying to manipulate or convert her into believing what he was writing. "Obviously I believe in God and that he wants a personal relationship with everyone, and that personal relationship is the highest thing I could wish for anyone else. However, the path to God has to be through each individual's own decisions and wishes."

He went on to tell Stine of their mutual friends who were Christians, and of Christian musicians they both liked. He invited her to continue their discussions of the meaning of life. "Hopefully I would be able to show you that Christianity is not about rules and regulations or about restrictions or straitjackets for people's expression. In reality, it's a source of freedom and creativity. Again, for me these things are so important, but I don't want them to come across as preachy. I want to share what I believe, and would very much like to hear your own reflections and thoughts on the greater meanings of life."

Thus began an e-mail conversation in which two friends talked about their joys and sorrows, their hopes and their questions about God and mankind, about religion and science, about truth, and about doubt.

Along the way Mikael recommended some outside reading material, not to take the place of their conversations but to supplement them. The first book was *Mere Christianity* by C. S. Lewis, and the other was *The Jesus I Never Knew* by Philip Yancey. Mikael and Stine discussed the issues that came up in the books, but the bulk of their conversations centered on their mutual interests, music, and friends.

By the middle of January, Stine wrote in an e-mail, "It's as though God has caught me by surprise. All those things I couldn't understand before have slowly, before my own eyes, become something I can grasp."

On March 9, Stine visited Copenhagen Vineyard for the first time. For the next couple of months, the e-mail conversation revolved around what she was experiencing at church, the Christians she was meeting, the pastor's sermons, and her growing understanding of God and faith.

On May 19 Stine e-mailed Mikael, "Yesterday was fantastic. . . . The teaching was so intense. I don't want to find myself in anything less than the state I was in yesterday. . . . If in reality that fantastic overwhelming sensation that touched me inside and filled me completely to the brim was God, then I hope he wants to come again. It was so beautiful. Just the thought of it brings butterflies to my stomach."

Two days later: Stine e-mailed Mikael:

Stine: Tra la la, today I have felt completely in love . . . all sorts of things are bubbling inside with excitement. But I guess that I really am. In love that is. You can relax. It's with Jesus.

Mikael: That's completely amazing, your new love. Congratulations. I think you'll make a great couple.[4]

E-mail has become an indispensable tool in any evangelistic strategy. Alex Demeshkin applies the principles of effectively using e-newsletters in an overall Internet evangelism plan. "In the commercial world, e-mail is considered to be the most cost-effective way to acquire new customers. Recent studies indicate that even in the religious category the percentage of e-mail marketing open rates and click-through rates is among the top four or five highest. A lot of people are using the Web for searching spiritual and religious information."

Sending e-mail costs you next to nothing because there is no printing or postage. It can be highly effective in an evangelistic outreach because it's measurable, as opposed to print where you don't know if the recipient read the mail or magazine piece or not.

As Mikael and Stine's story demonstrates, e-mail is potentially a lot more interactive. Through the relationships built in e-mail you can methodically persuade people to do something else—to get them to your Web site, to watch a video, to read a teaching or a Bible passage, to send a prayer request, to go to a Christian concert or event, or, as in the case of Stine, to visit a church.

So it can be a very effective strategy.

But as with every digital evangelism method, there are also things you will want to avoid with e-mail.

People like getting relevant e-mails from the people they know or from the organizations they know and trust. There is a negative attitude toward e-mail by many people, and rightfully so, because of the abuse by spammers.

"But there are several organizations that e-mail me on a daily, weekly, or monthly basis that I always read," Demeshkin observes, "and I save it because I know there is value in it. I know the names and I trust them. Try to establish that kind of a relationship with your audience and it can be used effectively."

NeedHim.com has also utilized e-mail effectively in its Internet evangelism strategy. "We added an e-mail response mechanism to the Web," NeedHim Ministries President Drew Dickens explains, "and that opened up a global response opportunity for us that we had not recognized before. Then we started having volunteers who not only could answer the phones but also respond to e-mail. And that was a huge bump for us in response. It was exciting because you would be e-mailing people from Bangladesh.

"There are some built-in frustrations," Dickens cautions. "E-mail can be slow. The recipients control the pace of it. You can pour your heart and soul into a response and never get anything back. You don't know what happened to them. That can be a little frustrating. But it is fun and it's exciting. E-mail is great for volunteers who are a little intimidated by the phone. They can put a little more thought into what they are going to say."[5]

Greg Outlaw from AllAboutGod.com explains the importance of follow up, through e-mail, instant messaging, or some other means. "You can also partner by answering e-mails or Instant-message back and forth. Obviously instant messaging is a little harder than answering e-mails. Answering e-mails can be done offline. You have plenty of time to think about what the person has written, and you can address it.

"With IM, you really need to be more knowledgeable or have access and fast typing on the computer to get the knowledge. You can go to AllAboutGod.com or other sites and search, get the information they're looking for and put it down.

"The best way to do e-mails is the personal touch, with a testimony. Be absolutely honest and authentic. I've seen God use that more than anything. Sometimes the best answer in the world is, 'I don't know; but I'll tell you this, I'll pray for you.' You can say, 'I'll think about it or I'll ask somebody, but I don't know. I'll get back to you.'

"You'd be surprised at how many people are blessed just to get a response at all," Outlaw explains, "because they usually get nothing or an automated response. So the personal touch is key. And it can't be just mush. It's got to be a place where you can deliver truth. Truth is the power of salvation.

"We have 45 people who answer e-mails on topics including testimonies, science and philosophy, religion—anything. Some of them are retired pastors, some are theologians or seminary graduates; some have no training whatsoever. They just know they can research one topic because they read God's Word and they know it. We check everything doctrinally, of course, before we send it out or publish it, because everything flows through us.

"We reached 197 countries, just in English, every month last year. I'm no different than a regular missionary. I was called to the nations, not just one—I was called to 197 last month. And these are the ones just in English. I'm working to get the whole thing in multiple languages.

"I believe that the Internet is the primary mission field of the twenty-first century. People will go to a search engine like Yahoo or Google and type something they would never ask their best friend or pastor or whomever else, but if you're there at the top, with truth, you'll be able to lead them to a relationship with Christ."[6]

Conversations 2.0: Message Boards, Chat, Text Messages

As we have seen, Web 2.0 is all about conversations. And most Internet evangelism happens through conversations and relationships built on the Web. So this is a wonderful moment in history when both the tools and the techniques are converging to create an atmosphere that's conducive to connecting with people and pointing them to Jesus. In addition to e-mail, other forms of online interaction include chat, instant messages, text messages (SMS), Skype (online telephone), and message boards or discussion forums. Here are some basic definitions:

- **Message Board**—A popular forum for conversation is a Web-based message center, where users post ideas, comments, questions, and responses.
- **Threaded Discussion**—An online dialogue in a series of linked messages. These threaded messages are created over time as users read and reply to each other's posts.
- **Newsgroup (Forum)**—An online discussion group dedicated to a particular subject of interest.
- **Chat**—Real-time communication over a computer network, involving at least two users usually typing text messages. Now the technology also exists for actual voice chat, and many Web sites are making this available.
- **Messaging**—A generic term referring to several modes and methods of online communication between people, including e-mail, message boards, Twitter, chat, instant messages, text

messages, newsgroup postings, and Internet telephone/video (Skype).

All of these methods are used effectively by NetCasters to win people to Christ online.

One group that has been hugely effective using chat and discussion boards for evangelism is Campus Crusade's TruthMedia. This group works to strategically build online communities of evangelism and discipleship and currently runs twenty-two Web sites in twelve languages. TruthMedia.com effectively uses chat, integrated and connected to other "felt-need" content within the site, to reach people with the gospel.

Karen Schenk, the director of TruthMedia, shares the strategy behind the ministry model. "It's a funnel that describes how the Web site goes from attracting visitors to ministering online. The top of the funnel is traffic coming to the Web site. That will usually be your largest number. Then we want our visitors to move deeper into the Web site. We'd like them to read articles that share the gospel. Our team puts a lot of emphasis on this.

"We want them to engage in community through chat or mentoring because we know at that point it'll become a deeper relationship with Christ as a result. Obviously we want them to make a decision."

Schenk explains that six areas of interactivity on TruthMedia.com move people toward making a decision for Christ:

Mentoring: "We don't look at mentoring as giving advice; we look at that as coming alongside of."

Prayer Mentoring: "We do this on our seeker sites. We ran a survey about prayer on one of our seeker sites, WomenTodayMagazine.com. We were just stunned at the results. Eighty percent of the people said they believed in prayer. I was devastated. I thought, 'We're reaching Christians. I don't want to be reaching Christians.' Then I read the next question. It said, 'To whom do you pray?' The responses were, to the goddess, to the winds, to the rains. I thought, 'Oh my goodness, this is wild.'

"We kept going through the survey results. In response to 'How often do you pray?' some people prayed once a day. Why do you pray?

'For good luck.' 'Because I have to.' 'Because . . .' There were all these ominous reasons.

"I said to our staff team, 'Let's try something crazy. Let's put a button on *WomenTodayMagazine* that says, 'Need prayer? Click here.' It seemed so radical, so 'Christian-ese.' Yet probably 20 to 30 percent of our e-mails from all our sites are from people wanting prayer."

Discussion Boards: "Moderated boards help give the opportunity to share thoughts and ideas to hear about the gospel. This is a great tool, but it is definitely wise to have somebody monitor them. We have a very unique one on our Web site, www.thelight.com. We've got Buddhists, we've got all kinds of different cults that meet in there; we have a high priestess, and a Satanist who tries to lead our discussion boards. We finally were able to find an apologist who would come and work on it, to tame it, because we really want to encourage them to talk, but we don't want them to convert other people the wrong way. So it's a real challenge to monitor that particular board, but it's also neat because you know the right people are on your site."

Follow-up Strategy: TruthMedia has developed a strategy that enables online follow-up for offline events. People at the event are informed that a particular person prayed to receive Christ, and on the comment card it says somebody will be following up on him or her through an e-mail. Mary Smith would then get an e-mail that would say, 'Dear Mary, thanks for coming to this event. We understand you just prayed to receive Christ. Here are some resources and some information.'

Within two to three days, she is then matched up with a mentor who contacts her by e-mail, and says, 'You have just indicated that you prayed to receive Christ. I'd like to help you.' The mentor offers online courses, indicating that there's a very basic discipleship one."

Online Courses: "We've created online courses as a discussion tool, not so much an answer. We have every topic from marriage to Bible studies. We'd like to think of it as a 'Chapters Online.' Whatever your area of interest is, you can find a little online course. It can be one lesson, or it could be eleven lessons long. Then those lessons get matched up with a study coach, and those two can interact. At the end of every lesson is a question about what are some concerns in your life, or how can I pray for you, which takes it to the spiritual dimension.

Chat Rooms: These forums exist on the sites to provide an arena where Bible-based evangelism and discipleship can occur in a safe and welcoming community. "We had a lot of suicidal people coming to our chat room for a while," Schenk explains. "We bought a search word, 'suicide', and it links to a life story that gives hope about suicide.

"So we met with a counselor and we came up with resources, all kinds of them. Now if you log into any of our chat rooms it says, 'Are you at the end of your rope?' and it links to a page that has a wealth of resources; and we want to connect them to a real community. Then our volunteers' role is just to come alongside and say, 'Let me pray for you, let me encourage you, this is where you need to go for help.' But then the volunteers don't have to carry that burden and feel like they need to save somebody's life that night. However, that being said, God has used us to save many, many lives.

"Just as people open up quicker on the Internet, you need to shut them down quicker. You just say, 'Can we stay focused? The reason we're here today is to discuss this topic, and I really want to discuss that with you. Let's stay focused, in fairness to all of the people who have taken the time to come here today.' So we just pull it in very quickly."[7]

Online chat is very fast paced, and it can be fun because it's so quick moving. It's not quite as fast as a phone conversation, so you can put a little thought into it. But it can also be difficult. It's one or two sentences back and forth in rapid-fire motion. This appeals to young people who like the feel of an online text conversation similar to real-time, face-to-face conversations.

Drew Dickens of Need Him Ministries explains that chat has become an important component of its overall ministry strategy. "Just on a whim we started chat. I have two teenage boys and they are huge into chat. So just for fun one night I Googled 'chat platforms.' I found some free open source code that would put a chat link on your site. It's nothing fancy, just a 'talk to me now' one-on-one customer service platform. We threw it up there and just got killed from all over the world.

"Ministries and individuals started copying the code and putting it on their sites, and it was just overwhelming. It was amazing. That was another big bump for us in our strategy, promoting ministries and individuals to add the link to their page. Chat was just huge for us.

"All our volunteers are trained to do phone, e-mail, and chat. All volunteers start monitoring a chat or a phone call. Most of them start by replying to an e-mail. It's slower, and they can put some thought into it. Then they move toward either phone or chat. Very few do both. They are different kinds of conversations. Chat's more youth-oriented and global, and you have to be a fast typist. So most of our chat volunteers are younger."

Another burgeoning avenue for digital ministry is telephone text messaging, or SMS, which has exploded in the United States and around the world.

Need Him is beginning to respond to text messages for some client ministries. "Most of our SMS that we are doing is for us and for the Palau Ministry who use SMS as an electronic reply card for festivals. So we have a five-digit code for them, just like how you vote on *American Idol*. We have a five-digit code that they promote from the stage, saying, 'Text your name to this code.' That way we electronically, immediately capture their name and their cell number. Then we call them back.

"We have a plan right now where people text in their name or send in an e-mail address and we respond to them that way. But SMS is really becoming a great opportunity."

"My son goes to Baylor," says Dickens, "and during the football game at halftime Sprint sponsors a publicity stunt where they encourage the students to take digital pictures of each other in the stands and then e-mail them through their cell phones to a number that Sprint puts on the scoreboard. Then at halftime they pick several of the goofy pictures and post them in full color up on the scoreboard for everyone to see.

"Nobody said, 'I can't imagine how that happened.' I'm blown away by the technology—how did that just happen? The students don't get freaked out about that. They did SMS, too. You text your name to a code and then during the third quarter they randomly pick a name from the database and you get a game ball. Think about what they captured from an acquisitions standpoint.

"I'll tell you who does a huge job of this is Bono of U2. While he is on tour he'll say, everyone in the concert, text your name to whatever, and you can come up on stage and I'll give you a T-shirt or whatever. All of a sudden you have twenty thousand kids all sending their name—and all of a sudden I'm going to be getting a text from Bono every day about world debt. It's brilliant. Again, he knows his audience."

There can be a downside to chat room ministry. Though you attract people who are seekers and you can enter into discussions with people, you may also encounter people who can be very antagonistic. Debra Brown of Hope House Church on Second Life had some negative experiences in chat rooms before she built her online church. "I would be talking and having a really good conversation with someone, and everyone was listening, because they are all in the same chat room. But then someone might chime in and say, 'She's an idiot. Who believes that? There is no truth. Who was Jesus anyway?'

"I've found that you get to know people in a chat room and then you send them an e-mail. I've found e-mail to be very effective because you have the time to sit down and think about it. You have a relationship. They give you their e-mail address and that's personal. It's more of a relational thing."

Stephen Shields oversees the American Bible Society's Faithmaps discussion group. "The one criterion for participation that is absolutely non-negotiable is respect. You can say anything, you can disagree with anything, but the one thing you can't do is . . . talk about people being stupid.

"When that happens in a discussion group you have a certain amount of power to stop that sort of thing because you can ban someone from your group or you can moderate all their messages, so you read all their messages before they get posted. . . . That's probably the best way to really get a discussion going.

"On the positive side there are people who are drawn to Internet participation in religious events because they're churchless Christians. . . ." Shields explained. "We have a number of folks in the Faithmaps discussion groups that just don't feel they have anywhere to turn, that don't have anywhere else to go, and they have developed a strong sense of online community where they are mutually accountable. Their self-perception is that's all they've got—that is their church. It's sad but that's the reality.

"Some people join and they're very bitter about the church. That has also segued into bitterness about God, but they're still sort of hungry and they want to try to differentiate that. So from a positive perspective, that's why some people tend to spend more time online."[8]

Blogs and Vlogs

One of the most effective means of reaching the world with the Word is currently through Internet conversation groups, including chat rooms, discussion boards, blogs, and vlogs (video blogs).

Blog is short for *Web log*, which is a type of online journal that has several key characteristics. Blogs are not meant to be merely articles. They are intended to be conversations and discussions. You as the blogger determine the topics. But then the ensuing discussions about the topic can take on a life of their own. Blogs are set up as reverse chronological posts, so that everything you publish to your blog is dated with the most recent entry always at the top of the page.

Another characteristic of a blog that you may or may not find on another type of Web site is the ability for commenting. A lively blog allows anybody on the Internet who comes across your post to respond to it, to correct you, to offer an opinion, or to add to the discussion.

Technorati is now tracking more than 70 million blogs, and approximately 120,000 new web logs are being created worldwide each day. That's about 1.4 blogs created every second of every day.[9]

At the Internet Evangelism in the 21st Century Conference at Liberty University, several experts on Web 2.0 gathered to discuss the revolutionary power of conversation on the Internet (http://ie-21stcentury.com.

"The anonymity of [the Internet] enables people to be more open than they normally would be," explains Steven Shields. "I say that the

Internet has an 'optional relationality.' If we meet on a discussion group and I don't like what he says, I can easily just leave the discussion group. If he and I exchange personal e-mails, I can write a rule in Outlook that will cause all of his e-mails to go right to my deleted folders.

"That being said, there can be a significant degree of intimacy that develops online—what I call a 'virtually unmediated relationship'—where you can get down to brass tacks and talk about each other's lives. The dynamic I've seen in our Faithmaps discussion groups we've had for the last four years is that people open up usually earlier and more intimately in an online environment than they would face-to-face, and then they get, as it were, 'tricked' into a genuine friendship, because as they develop a level of trust, the relationship can segue from online to real-time face-to-face.

"That is one way I think we need to look at blogging, at online—it's a segue ministry to try to help people transform and move into genuine face-to-face relationships."[10]

- "Seventy percent of blog readers are influentials, that is, people who are articulate and networked—the 10% of America who set the agenda for the other 90%" said D. J. Chuang, digital ministry architect at ForMinistry.com, an outreach of the American Bible Society. "So bloggers blog because they have something to say."
- "Often what you'll get is sub conversations where people will actually comment on the comments," declares Will Sampson, an independent technology consultant, and a blogger for the American Bible Society, "and begin to have a conversation within the comments themselves. So that gives you some context for what comments are."[11]
- "As bloggers link to each other, as we always tend to do, if you read somebody's blog you get to find about who they read and who their friends are, and you start to read them. So it starts to form this community, this group of people all talking about the same thing."[12]

Blogging experts recommend that you really consider what will allow the best conversation to take place. It's not only about publishing an article or a random thought and then getting people to read it. It's about creating an online space that allows for conversation, discussion, and debate to take place.

Active individual bloggers need two to three hours a day to maintain their content. Most bloggers use their own names, though some have blogged anonymously.

D. J. Chuang points out some of the benefits and the dangers. "It's become an individual communication tool which allows the fostering of transparency. This is a good thing and a scary thing at the same time because what you say instantly gets registered onto something like search engines. There's a search engine specifically for blogs, so if you say something about a product, an organization, or yourself, it's out there for the world to see.

"The publishing revolution that was started in the 1500s with the Gutenberg Press gave power and voice to the institution. Now blogging has given voice to the individual. You can instantly put your voice out, and if you have something to say and it shows up on people's radar, you can influence the world. You've seen the impact of blogging in politics, in media, and certainly in evangelism."[13]

Steve Knight started a reality television blog as a bridge strategy to investigate culture's fascination with reality television. "On my site I tie that into what Leonard Sweet calls EPIC, which stands for 'Experiential, Participatory, Image-based, and Connective.' That's an acronym he uses to talk about what our culture is searching for and how reality television really addresses a lot of those things. . . . It would be inauthentic of me to look at statistics and say, 'You know, there are millions of people who watch reality television shows. I don't watch reality television shows, but I want to reach people who watch reality television shows. So I'm going to start a reality television Web site and talk about that.' If it's not something that you're truly passionate about, it's going to quickly be discovered on the Web that this guy is really a ploy; this is a bait-and-switch situation.[14]

Some have become successful in blogging through a team effort. One excellent example of this is Allison Bottke's Boomer Babes blog (http://www.boomerbabesrock.com). Different boomer-age women take turns blogging on subjects of interest to them, and the comments are posted on Bottke's Web site.

While blogging remains popular, it's important to note that it can be all-consuming if you allow it to be, which can be dangerous to your health—both mental and physical. Tech researcher Gartner Inc. reported that in 2007, two hundred million people have given up blogging, more than twice as many as are active.

People who have blogged seriously for any length of time know it can have tremendous benefits, but it can also be a tremendous burden. "Good bloggers work like dogs," writes Michael Parsons, editor of the tech site CNet.co.uk. "You can't expect readers to show up unless you show up. And the Internet never closes. Every successful blogger I've come across is the same. Eat, sleep, and drink the work. No time out; no holidays."

In his article, "The Death of Blogs," Ted Olsen quoted Parsons and wrote, "That's not a recipe for healthy living, especially if you're working a day job that's not paying you to blog. When Catholic blogger Amy Welborn shut down Open Book . . . to focus on writing books, she wrote, 'I want to do good, and I want to do lasting good—the kind of good that people carry around, share, put on their bookshelves and reflect on—rather than the kind of good that sparks a momentary flash until we surf to the next Web site and the next and the next.'"[15]

While blogs remain popular, the explosive growth has leveled off. Today many who continue to blog do so because they have cornered the niche in their market or because they have a passion to chronicle their life experiences. Many who have begun blogging but did not attract a sizable audience have given up and moved on to other avenues of distribution. Others who began blogs have found it easier to use the tools and networking applications made available by social networks.

When I speak at Christian writers' conferences, I'm often asked my thoughts on blogging, whether I believe it's productive or a waste of time and energy. I answer that I do believe it's productive if you have name recognition or an outlet that will gather an audience for you. However, if someone doesn't have that name recognition or a platform from which to speak, I recommend the following:

- Consider linking up with an established ministry, writer, or speaker as a guest blogger.
- Focus on building a platform, with a blog as one plank in the structure from which to speak.
- Create a Blogger, MySpace, or Facebook page and a Twitter account and post thoughts via these avenues.
- Begin blogging but recognize that without name recognition there may be only a limited audience.
- Find another outlet for what the Lord would have you to say—radio, public speaking, television, etc.
- Learn more at the Internet Evangelism Day Web site section on blogs: http://www.internetevangelismday.com/blogging.php.

Vlogs and Vulnerability

Across the country, local churches and individual Web evangelists are catching the vision of using video blogs, or vlogs, to reach an online audience with the gospel. Two local churches that are making a significant impact on the Web are LifeChurch.tv and Flamingo Road Church in Florida.

LifeChurch.tv

LifeChurch.tv is an innovative ministry that grew out of Edmond, Oklahoma. Every week the various satellite campuses across America join together—along with online viewers around the world on Second Life, Facebook, and LifeChurch.tv—to worship God and to experience truths from the Bible. Satellite broadcasts enable all the local brick-and-mortar locations to be connected in one worship experience. LifeChurch.tv is a multisite church that transcends metropolitan regions.

In April 2007, LifeChurch.tv launched its fully interactive campus in Second Life, the popular 3-D online virtual world. Currently LifeChurch.tv is hosting nearly twenty-thousand people every weekend across all its campuses during forty-seven worship experiences.[16]

Flamingo Road Church

In fall 2007 the pastor of Flamingo Road Church in Florida, Troy Gramling, decided to "get naked" on the Internet. In an innovative Web outreach, Pastor Gramling allowed himself to be watched via his video Web blog on a twenty-four-hour Web cam in four locations: his house, car, hotel, and office. Every day, all day, Internet viewers saw his life in a fishbowl—the good, the bad, the great, and the ugly.

Why did he do this? As his video log explained, "We are all fish in a bowl. The more transparent (naked) we get, the more God can do amazing things through us." The outreach received worldwide attention in the media, attracting thousands to his online evangelism ministry, including an online congregation.[17]

Text-based Articles and Internet Evangelism

Despite all the advances in Web 2.0 technology, video, and mobile, Tony Whittaker sees online text as indispensable. "I think written words remain a core tool of communication and hopefully always will. Online text still has a vital role for clear communication. But audio and video are increasingly strategic too."

While the communication elements of Web 2.0 allow for conversations online, and video offers attention-grabbing clips, text articles and in-depth teaching allow the serious seeker the opportunity to "go deep" in a quest for truth. This is especially attractive to the more intellectual and mature seeker comparing various religions. Apologetic Web sites have been very effective in reaching this type of seeker.

While praising the growth of video online, online evangelist James Watkins warns ministries and individual Internet evangelists to resist the urge of moving away from the use of text on their Web sites. "I'm sure that the video is nice for people who don't like to read or who don't have a lot of time. But for somebody who wants a bit of information, who wants a sound bite, or who wants a quote to cut and paste and put into an article—I want to be able to go to the actual print, to cut and paste, and glance through it and find the particular bit I'm looking for.

"I've always been a news junkie. So I think being able to combine news events and my faith is just ideal. The gospel of John, chapter 1, describes Jesus as being full of truth and grace. I've tried to keep that in mind. Yeah, I want to tackle the topics, but I want to do it with grace. I've got an article called 'God Hates GodHatesFags.com.' I have my response to this infamous article and just how unbiblical and un-Christian it is. I had this very outspoken homosexual leader write me: 'I may not agree with everything you say on your site, but if there is a God, I hope that He's the God that you describe.'

"I have another testimony of a woman who came to my Web site. She just happened to type 'love' into Google. That mine would pop up in the first one hundred pages is really amazing. I think it's a real God thing. She said that she got into it and was kind of cynical. She thought, 'This is some sort of Bible thing and they're trying to get people to convert.' But she said, 'My hand was frozen to the remote.' And her last line was, 'Do you think that God was trying to tell me something?'

"There was another gal who said, 'Your site saved my life tonight.'"

Internet evangelist Rusty Wright has also seen dramatic results of his targeted text-based articles, which are now posted on more than three hundred Web sites, both Christian and secular, around the world—and can be found in more than thirteen languages.

"There is a Nigerian man living in Belgium, and he is sitting in front of his computer and he's watching a pornographic video. And then he has this idea, to focus on the concept of love. 'My spirit tells me, *love*,' he wrote, 'so I decided to log on to Google and type in *the secret of love*.' He found one of my columns that is basically an evangelistic article talking about love, relationships, and premarital sex. At the end it brings in Jesus.

"'When I read it I felt different,' he explained. 'I asked myself, why do I always think about sex every day? This has affected me negatively. I promise myself never to watch porno films again, but to walk in the commandment of God. I thank God for using you.'"

Wright crafts his articles considering both the intellectual and the "felt needs" of his audience. "I try to find out what's going on inside the mind and heart of the nonbeliever and then use that as an entry point for spiritual truth and the gospel. But my approach is not just to write articles to meet needs that people feel they have, in other words, just to make them feel better or just to have a better relationship or be more successful, although those things are important. But what I try to do is use the felt need as an entry point into a real need.

"We all have felt needs. For some it might be an extra chocolate dessert or a million dollars or to be number one in their class or number one in business. But we know that people also have real needs—food, water, air, and, of course, spiritually, eternal life, you need Jesus.

"My task as an outreach Christian communicator, I believe, is to find the felt needs people have and see how I can use that as an entry way to their heart to show them the importance of Scripture. Just like that Nigerian guy who at first was interested in sex and then he was interested in love and he started reading my article, and it brought him to realizing that human beings have three dimensions—physical, psychological, and spiritual—and you need to focus on all three. Then it talked about how to develop the spiritual dimension and talked about Christ.

"Sometimes I use traditional apologetics for that, for instance when people have questions about the reliability of the Bible or the Resurrection or whatever. But also I would use what I call cultural apologetics, which is using elements of culture, especially popular culture, to point people to spiritual truth."

Advanced NetCasting

We've discussed e-mail, chat, blogs, and text. Now it's time to move on to the next level in the convergence of media that we call the Internet—online video!

Chapter Five

FishTube: Video and Internet Evangelism

Another method of connecting with seekers is through short- and long-form video, both amateur and professional. Since Broadband exceeded 50 percent penetration in the U.S. market in 2004, online video has exploded in popularity. The *Los Angeles Times* reported a survey by the nonprofit Conference Board showing that nearly a quarter of households in the United States now view television programs online. The quarterly Consumer Internet Barometer survey found that news shows were watched by 43 percent of online viewers, followed by sitcoms, comedies, and dramas, watched by 35 percent. Slightly less than 20 percent viewed reality shows online, and 18 percent took in sports.

The survey found that 90 percent of online viewers watch at home. The remaining 10 percent watch at the office.[1]

According to Microsoft founder Bill Gates, the Internet is set to revolutionize television viewing, as a result of an explosion of online video content and the merging of PCs and television sets.[2]

Gates predicts that in the years ahead, audiences will demand the flexibility offered by online video and abandon conventional broadcast television, with its fixed program slots and advertisements that interrupt shows. "Certain things like elections or the Olympics really point out how TV is terrible. You have to wait for the guy to talk about the thing you care about or you miss the event and want to go back and see it," he said. "Internet presentation of these things is vastly superior. Because TV is moving into being delivered over the Internet—and some of the big phone companies are building up the infrastructure for that—you're going to have that experience all together," Gates said.[3]

The rise of high-speed Internet and the popularity of video sites like YouTube and Tangle have already led to a worldwide decline in the number of hours spent by people in front of a TV set. eMarketer reports that according to the Global Web Index, from Trendstream, with research conducted by Lightspeed Research, 72 percent of U.S. Internet users watch video clips monthly—making video bigger than blogging or social networking.[4]

The U.S. television audience was twice the size of its broadband Internet population in 2006. But according to eMarketer, by 2011, America's broadband audience is likely to swell to two-thirds that of TV. Three-quarters of online video viewers watched more video in 2007 than they did in 2006, and more than one-half expected to watch even more in 2008, according to a study conducted by Taylor Nelson Sofres and sponsored by AOL and Google. Analysts at eMarketer estimate that in 2006 114.3 million Americans were watching video on the Internet. By 2011 that audience is expected to increase by 50 percent to 183 million viewers.[5]

E-Marketing.com's Alexander Castro observes, "In the past year, online video has graduated beyond amateur, user-generated content to now include professionally produced series created specifically for the Web. . . . New video search technologies have been developed that allow Web users to search inside a video or audio file for specific keywords and topics before consuming the entire clip. The targeting potential for advertisers is enormous."[6]

Online Video and Internet Evangelism

With this new interest in online video, and the new search capabilities, the targeting potential for Internet evangelism is equally enormous.

"Video has a unique ability," says Alex Demeshkin, "Just like when we communicate, it's in the gestures, facial expressions, and other things that video communicates. It is strong and effective, like you're present there with them. That's why video is so unique and so important."

The exciting thing about the digital video revolution is it's also affordable to an individual NetCaster, a local church, or a small parachurch ministry. You don't need high-end production quality of videos to get started. You don't have to purchase a $20,000 dollar professional camera or lights. With the advance of digital video technology, today you can merely grab a simple webcam or a regular consumer type camera and start shooting video.

And the good news is that your typical Web users today are OK with that because they're used to YouTube, which has a lot of low-quality, low-production value material. So if you have a message that really engages people, you can broadcast events very easily.

The most popular online videos are not the slick, professional production pieces that you see on TV. They are typically amateur clips of people being creative.

Jesse Carey of Relevant online believes that if people can tap into that creative energy in an evangelistic sense, they won't have to have the resources of a production team or a video crew. "What people are looking for is authenticity. They like video bloggers. I think if you can adopt that appeal of the online video, then it can definitely be, in terms of new trends, something to try to work outward."

The key is creative thinking and singleness of purpose.

Carey points to a YouTube group that actually started as a group of atheists. "They wanted to get people to submit and upload YouTube videos of them committing blasphemy of the Holy Spirit. That caused a lot of buzz. It had the potential to be a wake-up call to some Christians."

The atheists were invited by Way of the Master, with Ray Comfort, to have a debate, and it ended up on ABC's Nightline. It was a relatively civil and engaging debate. But if it wasn't for those YouTube videos, few people would have seen that there are this many atheists who are willing to do this. "In a way they figured out a way to execute what they wanted to in an anti-religious way. It ended up that there was a positive outcome to that."

Dumpster Diving for Gold

But Johnnie Gnanamanickam of CBN.com cautions that working with video has a downside as well as its positive side, both for users and for online evangelists.

"Video is a tough one, especially with YouTube, and Tangle, and places like that. Someone said that it's like 'Dumpster diving for gold.' You have, I wouldn't even say a wealth—it's more like a garbage Dumpster full of stuff. Helping people find what they need and getting down to it, that's really a challenge."

But Johnnie points out that there is a way to make video workable for evangelism. "One of the things that I think would be cool is to bring the interactive element into it. We need to start doing interactive live shows and things like that on video. Tangle lets you do a Web camera or a text chat to talk. I think that's going to start being popular. You can build an audience and do interactive Internet video shows. That would probably be productive, especially if you are answering questions."

Along with his work as an Internet consultant and architect, Richard Helsby has worked with the popular Christian video program OneCubed.com. He explains how Internet evangelists can utilize video effectively: "You can do something very powerfully visually. I think most people now have been forwarded a clip of something. As certain clips are developed and created, they can be passed around and shared and put into spaces where you never know who might see them. You see the popularity of certain clips, whether it be on YouTube or things like that. So creative clips that connect with people and reveal deeper truths hold tremendous potential."

"Pretty much everything that is out there at the moment is all short-form—two to three minutes. Most people just snack on the video. Things are going long-form as people are starting to watch some of their TV shows out there. Most people aren't going to go watch a whole bunch of shows that they don't know about, unless they're really interested in them. I can see long-form things taking hold as well, but that would be the next stage, if people are really interested in something. It could be meeting a certain need or a certain piece of information that they're looking for—maybe they'll watch something that's longer.

"But if you're doing that initial evangelism, and you're aiming at them, there will be the short-forms, the trailers, the ideas, and the concepts.

"God works in people, like the sower sowing the seed. Some seeds take and some don't. It's kind of a process and a journey for some people. So you can design video that starts saying, 'Hey, maybe there's something out there apart from what you just see.' Start seeding that idea and putting that in video, in short-form on YouTube.

"But the community decides what's popular. That's the interesting thing. You then have the question of 'Once I finish watching the clip, then what?' So you have to think through that."

The next step in the process is to move a viewer to a gospel presentation of some sort. This might be a video, a text explanation of the plan of salvation, or a flash presentation of some sort. Or you might move him into a chat, instant message, or Skype environment where someone can lead him in a prayer of salvation.

Once a person makes a commitment to Jesus Christ through one of these methods, there must be a strategy for discipleship and encouraging him to become a part of a local church.

"Try to plug people into a community," Helsby suggests. "If you can get communities where people can be nurtured and grow, plug them in there. Plug them into an online course where they can choose what's relevant. Ideally, if you can get multiple people taking that course at the same time—with human interaction and facilitators—there are huge networking possibilities and potential."

But it takes people. God will typically work through people having relationships with other people. There is a need for a facilitator, and that's where local churches can get involved. By building relationships first online, people don't have to come to the building. It's less threatening. Hopefully they will check out a church online and build a relationship. Once trust is built, they may be willing to visit the church in person.

Alex Demeshkin encourages NetCasters to harness the power of synergizing different elements of outreach with video online. "If you're working with a typical Internet audience, a mixture of combining marketing techniques, including Internet and using different channels, is a very good strategy. So if you have a TV program or a radio show or a print publication, cross-selling is very effective. The synergy is so great.

"For example, you hear a commercial and it says, 'Call now,' and they give a long phone number that has a lot of digits. You may or may not remember it because you are driving and you don't have a pen to write it down, even if it's something you're looking for. If the radio says, 'Are you having a struggle with an issue?' And it talks about Christianity and church and says, 'To find out more and find a local group that meets here locally, go to something like www.needhim.com,' that's logical and easy to remember. Chances are the listener is going to go when they are at their computer and jump on that Web site. So here you have the synergy of these two things working together."

Demeshkin also points to the future power of IPTV, which is television on the Internet, becoming mainstream in the United States. "Basically, think of IPTV as an interactive TV. It not only allows you, like TiVo or DVRs, to stop, pause, record, playback, and so on, but also have all of the good interactive functionality that the Internet has embedded into that television set. You may be watching a historic channel about biblical archaeology, and it talks about the Dead Sea Scrolls. If you're really interested in the subject, you can stop it right there and start reading off the Internet on the topic."

There are endless possibilities for video online today. Churches are streaming services or individual sermons; NetCasters are posting individual testimonies with a gospel message attached; young and old alike are posting creative short-play videos of two or three minutes that capture the attention of Web surfers; and flash designers are creating gospel presentations that include animated graphics and video elements.

The future of video on the Web is truly exciting, and limited only to the creativity of the individual NetCaster.

Podcasting

Video, along with audio, begs for portability. People don't want to be tethered to their desktops. That's why Apple's iPhone and digital devices like it are becoming so popular. "Ever since podcasting was introduced, the question has been the same: Will anyone listen? The answer is definitely, 'Yes,'" says Paul Verna of eMarketer, who estimates that the total U.S. podcast audience reached 18.5 million in 2007. Furthermore, that audience will increase by 251 percent to 65 million in 2012. And of those listeners, 25 million will be "active" users who tune in at least once a week. "As the U.S. podcasting industry matures it is unquestionably creating a listening audience."[7]

Verna is an eMarketer senior analyst and the author of the report, "Podcast Audience: Seeking Riches in Niches." He points out that a number of factors are driving the growth of the podcast user base, including greater ease of consumption for podcast content, growing awareness of podcasting, terrestrial radio's use and promotion of podcasting, increased penetration of portable players, and the evolution of smart phones, and proliferation of affordable mobile data plans.

"No one will argue that mobile devices and communication are becoming widespread," says Verna. "Even so, the majority of podcasts are actually experienced on PCs, not portable devices." The situation might change in time, but for now podcasts are mainly a desktop phenomenon as opposed to a mobile or portable one.[8]

Tony Whittaker points out the strength of podcasting as an element of effective Internet outreach: "The MP3 is great for music and also short or long audio clips. And, of course, with mobile phones increasingly turning into MP3 players, too, the potential for download-able audio presentations of different sorts to take with you and listen to when traveling, or whenever, is certainly significant."[9]

Jesse Carey also sees great potential for podcasting. "I think pod-casting is hugely effective. People can download it and listen to it when they want. Whereas with other types of media, they had to knowingly turn on the channel and be there at a certain time, or they had to turn on the radio. The Web 2.0 thing kind of started with putting media in the user's terms. They can take the podcast with them wherever they go. They can listen to it whenever they want on their iPod."[10]

What's Now? What's Next?

All of these methods are being used effectively by NetCasters around the world. Now, with the advent of social networks like Facebook, MySpace, and others like them, these techniques are being implemented in ways that have far-reaching implications for Internet evangelism. Let's look at how NetCasters can use these social networks to connect with people and point them to the answers.

Chapter Six

Gathering in the Aquarium: Social Networks and Internet Evangelism

L eading experts have called the social network explosion the second phase of the Internet's development. As I mentioned earlier, some of the leading social networks are among the twenty most popular Web sites in the world.

A social network is a Web site that provides a virtual community for people interested in a particular subject or a location to hang out together. Members create their own online profile with biographical data, pictures, likes, dislikes, and any other information they choose to post. They communicate with each other by voice, chat, instant message, video conference, and blogs. The social network typically provides a way for members to easily contact friends of other members.

During the past few years, social networking has exploded across the globe, confirming that this phenomenon is not just a fad. Social networks have now become central to the new Internet experience.

According to the Pew study on teens and social networks, 64 percent of online teenagers ages twelve to seventeen post content on social networks. The survey found that content creation is not only about sharing creative output, it is also about participating in conversations fueled by that content. Nearly half (47 percent) of online teens have posted photos where others can see them, and 89 percent of those teens who post photos say that people comment on the images at least "some of the time."[1]

RelevantMagazine.com Managing Editor Jesse Carey says that young people are coming up with creative ways to use social networks to share their faith. "I think it's an extension of how they communicate in general. For people who are really comfortable sharing their faith in normal situations, you can literally see it by going into their Facebook or their MySpace. A lot of times people can post files about themselves, have their quotes, or they can have worship songs playing. They can be very direct."

Social networks are an exciting tool to aid NetCasters in reaching seekers online. Whether NetCasters are trying to organize an event, or get people together and spread a message, social networking can help make that happen.

South African Internet consultant Richard Helsby sees much promise in social networking. "It allows you to do evangelism by working within community. You've got people who are discussing and interacting. You can connect with groups of people you normally couldn't connect with."

What makes social networks effective for Internet evangelism is that conversations are taking place and relationships are being built. Someone may be attracted by a video or an article or some sort of felt need being met. Once they are in the social network, evangelism happens person-to-person as it does in real life

"Probably the most effective thing is when people move into other people's communities," Helsby explains, "which is exactly the same model as real life. So you've got these communities, and then you can dialogue and get to know people. That's a long process, building those relationships and getting to know the people you're interacting with."

Typically, a person doesn't stumble onto a social network or Internet evangelism site, look around, and in one day receive Christ. In most cases Internet evangelism is only one piece of all the things that God is using to touch their lives. It's the same in real life. Most of those initiatives are effective because a friend is bringing a friend. So it comes down to relationships.

God works differently in each individual. It all depends on where a person is in the process of seeking truth. Somebody may be more intellectual, so maybe an apologetic site would lead her to Christ. Another person may be very relational, so a social network with chat or instant messaging may be the best way to reach him.

"God is the one who calls someone," says Helsby. "But in most cases, it's up to us to approach them and tell them the Good News. So now the Internet is just another way to do that."

Facebook, MySpace, YouTube, and Tangle

MySpace is only one of dozens of social networks that are letting people have a voice on the Web. Other sites include Facebook, Classmates, MSN Spaces, Xanga, Yahoo! 360, Flickr.com, Friendster, Bebo, Tagworld and many more. And now there are a myriad of Christian, filtered social networks like My.CBN.com, MeetFish, My Christian Space, MyPraize, and others. Teen Mania has created a filtered discipleship social network called MyBattleCry where young people can meet, interact, and keep track of their Bible reading and prayer life. Video social networks like YouTube and the Christian site Tangle have also become increasingly popular.

My local church in Chesapeake, Virginia, uses Tangle because it's free and it doesn't have the objectionable material you would find on YouTube. Our young-adult minister has been collecting video testimonies and posting them on Tangle and also on a Facebook testimony page.

Facebook has exploded in growth recently, in part because it has hundreds of free applications that are perfect for helping people to connect including chat, online conferences, short-play video, and detailed event invitations. Facebook also enables you to interconnect with different groups both locally and worldwide.

The selling points of Facebook include:

- It's fast;
- It's free;
- It's viral;
- It has a plethora of tools and applications for connecting;
- It engages the younger generation.

Communication expert Cynthia Ware of thedigitalsanctuary.org shares ten simple steps to get you started in social networking:

1. Repent! Realize you've been apathetic or cynical about social media because, well, mainly because people put down what they don't understand. Rethink; go another way.
2. Join Facebook. Signing up is easy and free. All you need is an e-mail address and a desire to build relationships.
3. Create your personal profile. This can be as simple or complex as you like. It can take as little as five minutes, or you can get wordy.
4. Invite your friends to add you. Searching for your friends is very easy, especially if someone you know has already added many of your acquaintances.
5. Join groups that reflect parts of you, your interests, profession, education, geographic area, etc. Anything you find interesting will connect you with others.
6. Feed your page. If you also blog, make sure you syndicate your content with RSS (a dialect of XML format) which for Facebook is easy to use. Try Blog Really Simple Syndication (RSS) Feed Reader.
7. Mingle on purpose. Remember you want to connect with friends but also stretch beyond the familiar.
8. Add events you think others might be interested in hearing about or attending. Anything counts—seminars, financial classes, scrapbooking parties, etc.

9. Create a group. The options are endless. I've seen unique examples including genealogy groups, reunion groups, memorial groups, etc.

10. Check your page at regular intervals. Use it or lose it. If you don't check in and respond, people will lose interest in their ability to connect with you. Plus, your home page is where the news feed lives. It's how you get current information on all the people you want to be connected with.[2]

Overcoming Hindrances to Social Network Evangelism

Richard Helsby is mindful that individual Christians must rise up to do the work of evangelism online. "You've got to overcome the obstacles that are preventing people from doing it, much like if you have a person sitting in the pew who doesn't evangelize in the real world. It takes people out of their comfort zone a little bit. You'd have to model Internet evangelism for people so that they can see how it can take place. You can give an example of what happened in a discussion forum or in Second Life. You can give testimonies of what you did with your church. It's important to give practical examples. People aren't going to be aware of all the various methods available to them.

"'How do I evangelize in Facebook?' they may ask. What's a subtle approach? Use this application on your profile and it will pop up this gospel presentation and it might get people interested. Show the steps to be able to do it—and be continually equipping and training others to do evangelism online."

Helsby also points out the power of online video. "Creative clips that connect with people and reveal deeper truths hold tremendous potential. As certain clips are developed and created, they can be shared and put into spaces where you never know who might see them."

But beyond video there must be the next step in the process. You might be able to draw seekers in with video. But there must be something beyond that, not only for evangelism but also for discipleship.

"Get those fundamentals and then start simple with what you can do," says NetCaster John Edmiston. "If people don't want to do all the

Web pages and they don't want to buy Dreamweaver, they may want to just go to a social networking site. Or if they're a video kind of person, do short videos on YouTube—stuff that's a little bit quirky and humorous. Make it tie in to a particular search. 'Funny Video' will bring up one hundred fifty thousand videos. But 'Funny Video' about something very specific that someone types in will attract people searching on the Web.

"One of the things with communities like MySpace is that we're moving from the one-to-many, to the many-to-many," Edmiston observes. "So someone says something, and someone else chimes in, and they all have a big discussion about it. With the postmodern distrust of a single point of authority, I think if you can get communities that can share Christ, it becomes the many-to-many interaction. That may be a very powerful form of evangelism for the postmoderns."

Helsby sees the relational aspects of the Web 2.0 concept as vital for the future of Web evangelism. "Internet evangelism uses the power of community. How can we facilitate Christians to contribute to evangelism—and make it easy for them? How do we say, 'OK, it's not just the pastor now?' How can I encourage them to be part of this movement? How can I leverage the network effect?

"We need to be thinking through strategies for enabling the masses to use the Internet for evangelism. I can create a MySpace profile and choose a Christian theme, maybe. The trend is in building applications for your profile. But how about applications that are evangelistic? What can I do that enables this person to do some kind of application that reaches out to other people, connects with friends, or in a nonthreatening way puts truth out there?

"Some could be fun. Some could be games or true-and-false questions. Who knows? You can get creative. When I add a photo on my Facebook profile, my friends are all told 'Richard now has a new photo; go have a look.' Now if I had an application, 'Richard is taking the "Do You Know What Christianity Is?" course,' all my friends are going to see that. Or make it more subtle: 'Richard is taking "Do You Know Your Purpose for Living" course,' and they click on that and say, 'Oh, this is interesting.'"

The key is to enable each person with tools and applications to do Internet evangelism and to reach his friends by taking advantage of the network effect.

According to RelevantMagazine.com Managing Editor Jesse Carey, where the rubber meets the road in Internet evangelism is the willingness to be engaged in Internet relationships.

"It really comes down to basic stuff. Answer e-mails. Foster a community where if someone has questions they can get answers from someone. Whether you have to develop a MySpace group, a Facebook group, a network, or a message board, people are on the Internet for the content because they want to engage with it. That has to be knowingly fostered for it to work. This is especially true with evangelism, because there is so much followership—if you want to make it more than a conversion—if you want to really make a disciple.

"If they want something that they can be detached from, there are tons of things. They can read books. They can read a magazine. Or they can tune into a program. But if they want something that offers complete transparency—that they can interact with, that they can be a part of the community—then that's when they're going to plug in to something online, and that's where online evangelism comes in.

"So I would say, know that it's not just about the content, it's about the community. If you're putting this message out there, be ready for feedback. Be equipped to answer it. Or if you can't personally answer it, be equipped to provide answers. The community is where everything happens."

Second Life

One of the more fascinating developments in social networking has been the creation of Second Life. Second Life is a 3-D virtual universe created and maintained by the member "residents" who join and create their own online personas through "avatars." Debra Brown serves on the executive board of the Digital Evangelism Network. As her culminating project for her MDiv at Gordon-Conwell Seminary, Brown decided to create an evangelism-oriented church, Hope House, which is literally located in the clouds of Second Life.

Debra asked her son-in-law for ideas for her project and he suggested Second Life. "I asked, 'What is Second Life?' So he showed me online, and I said, 'This is so cool. I can't build this church, but will you help me with it?' I showed him a picture of Calvary Church in Charlotte, and that just inspired him for this church in the clouds, with all the glass.

"I think the Second Life experience is really the next generation of Internet evangelism. A lot of the Internet evangelism that you have now is one way. It's a post. It's a Web site. It's a video. It's an MP3. I'm telling you something and you have no ability to respond to me.

"Chat rooms are a little less like that. But often in the chat rooms there are so many people and you can't really get deep with them. So it's more like talking at somebody. But with Second Life, it's an interaction—it's not static. So it's not like you're saying, 'I have something I want to communicate with you, and you really need to have this. So here it is, and here are the four spiritual laws. Here's the story of Jesus and you should listen to it.' It's not like that. It's building online relationships."

Second Life is another creative way that the church can empower the saints to do ministry online.

"On Second Life I have another property that someone donated to me," Brown explains. "They said, 'You're doing some really neat things. I thought you could use this property.' So I went shopping on Second Life and found a do-it-yourself building at an architecture store. I bought it with 400 Lindens, which is like nine bucks or something. I went to put it on the property—click this, click that, and the next thing you know I've got a building on a piece of property. And I'll use that for a Christian resource center. I'm going to fill it with Bibles and T-shirts, things like that.

"I have monthly fees, because of the bandwidth I use. But I think it's about twenty nine bucks a month for my presence on Second Life."

The potential for ministry through Second Life and social networks like it is great because it's fun, it's different, and the average person in the average church can do it with very little investment and training.

"Actually, they can do it for free," Brown says, "because they can just come and be a part of our congregation, or anyone's ministry on Second Life. You can just go and hang out. Second Life is relational. You are meeting a person, and you get to know them. People are being saved all the time online.

"People see the pastor name over my head and they come into the church and are willing to chat with me. The thing that surprised me is that people look at that name—pastor—and it means something to them. They either get angry and start attacking Christianity, or they will engage in a conversation.

"The first question they ask me is, 'Are you a R. L. pastor (a real-life pastor) or just Second Life?' They are looking for my credentials. They want to know if they can trust me. They want to know if they tell me something, am I going to tell somebody else. They want to know if I'm going to give them some spiritual answer, because often I think they are hoping that I will. They want to make sure they can trust it."

At Hope House Debra conducts Bible studies and preaches sermons. But the church is set up so that she doesn't have to be there at all times. So a seeker can go into the church and can hear the gospel message. He can read it or download the sermon podcasts.

"My best ministry happens when I just go and sit in there and I deal with somebody one-on-one. Really, that's when it happens. You have it a little bit when there is a group, and you have thirty avatars, and you preach, and they are saying, 'Amen.' Or I can hang out in there, do some work on the side, somebody comes along and I can touch their heart in a one-on-one conversation and they are changed. That's a different kind of church."

Christian Social Networks

John Sorensen is vice president at Evangelism Explosion and serves on the executive board of the Digital Evangelism Network. He recognizes that social networks are emerging as a significant way to reach young people with the gospel. Working with a focus group of young people in their teens and twenties, Sorensen created the XEE social network version of Evangelism Explosion for Generation X and Generation Y. This will be used as part of the training process for Evangelism Explosion (EE), because younger people tend to learn something, and then use the Web to learn more, dig deeper, and go further.

"Our plan is to build at least three elements within the XEE Web site," Sorensen explains. "We're going to have a testimony builder site that young Internet evangelists can use, not only to build their testimony, but then to share it with friends. We want to begin to include this as a big piece of who these young people are, so that they're identified as having that testimony.

"The second thing is this incredibly rich Web site where they are talking about concepts in discussion groups within the class sessions themselves. They can go back on the Web and they can learn more about any of these areas. We won't be covering them to the depth within the classes that we would have tried to do with adults before, because we know they'll learn more, and they'll add more, and they'll get more on the Web.

"Then the third element is we're going to actually try to create a community where mentoring can happen. Within that will be how to witness, and how to go further with that training. So there are really those three pieces that we're going to make sure that this XEE Web site has."

Dr. Sterling Huston serves on the board of Evangelism Explosion and has also expressed enthusiasm for this new XEE initiative. "It was created by consulting with a lot of Gen-X-ers around Europe and from other developing nations. You should hear the enthusiasm of these people in this age group who are saying, 'I have a way now to begin conversations with people in my group who I feel totally comfortable with. It has opened up new communication with my family, with my friends, with those I meet at Starbucks, wherever it might be.'

"This is the kind of tool that new generations are going to feel very comfortable with—they won't be apologizing for. If they have a heart to share their faith, it gives them a door opener and conversation starter to do that."

Rather than building a social network around XEE, Evangelism Explosion plans to integrate into other social networks like Facebook or the Christian site MeetFish.

"We adults use the Internet as a tool," Sorensen explains, "sending e-mail, Web browsing to look at news, and things such as that. Kids live on the Web. There was a recent news story of kids in today's world, and we're talking age fifteen and under. They will instant message somebody else sitting in the same room rather than have a face-to-face conversation.

"I'll walk into my son's room in the evening, and he'll have ten instant messages open at one time. One of them is an audio session, and he's talking with a friend who has moved away. Then he'll have nine others open, and he met these kids through playing an online game. He got to know them, they instant message, and they talk about all kinds of things. That's the world that we live in today.

"I'm excited about XEE," says Sorensen. "But I'm more excited about the change it represents in creativity for the ministry of Evangelism Explosion. We're going to release it to the world. And I hope and pray that we get thousands and thousands of kids worldwide who are ready to share their faith."

Diving In to the Social Network Community

The key for you, as you consider answering God's call to be a NetCaster for Christ through social networks, is to begin at the beginning.

"To start with, that person needs to just take the dive," says Johnnie Gnanamanickam of CBN.com. "Get a Facebook account. If you're scared of MySpace, OK, leave MySpace alone. But at least get a Facebook account. Start adding contacts. Dive in, figure out how it works, and start living there.

"Get a mobile device that has Internet access. I highly recommend an unlimited data access plan so you can get in there and see what you can do. Get familiar, get comfortable. Start not only connecting with people you know and have known, but look for opportunities to network, reach out, and grow that list.

"Start getting comfortable with building relationships online."

It's probably more powerful to do this as a team. Gnanamanickam suggests gathering a team of people together, setting up a group, and feeding off one another. Everybody brings their strength to the table. Somebody might be strong in video, somebody might be a writer, somebody else might be technical. Use your team to talk about your special interests or hobbies, to connect with other people. Regardless of a person's religious beliefs, this kind of affinity outreach gives people a place to start talking. Whatever your interests may be, add them to your MySpace or Facebook account. Start blogs on the stuff that you do that other people would be interested in reading.

For organizations wanting to do Internet evangelism, Gnanamanickam suggests that they concentrate on building tools. "On Facebook, for instance, there's a lack of evangelistic or Christian applications. For organizations and churches that can do it, I'd say focus on building applications that you and other Christians can use."

"You now have the potential, if you can build it, to create an international community of young Christians, multi-languages, who are dialoging and who are getting introduced to the gospel through music or video, and then are being discipled and helped to grow and live it out," says South African Internet evangelist Richard Helsby who works with One Cubed, a Christian music and culture television show. "I can't go to all of those countries. I can't connect to all those folks. But now we have the ability to network all of them together, to enable them to encourage one another. It's still got to be built—but the potential is there. There's no reason it can't be done.

"This Internet trend of community is amazing, because that's a key component of Christianity. I'd say that Internet evangelism has huge potential. But I would say we need to figure out a way to enable Christians to use it and be effective in it. We need to equip and enable, make it easy, get them to understand it and move into those places."

Helsby stresses the need to point people to the local church once you've witnessed to them online. "Don't separate it from your relational, one-on-one, face-to-face evangelism. I'd say that we've, as a whole, given over our responsibility to these media—these tools. 'I don't need to speak to my neighbor; they can watch the Christian TV show—they can read that book. I don't need to speak to my neighbor; they can go online.' We've given it over to a tool, but a tool is not a person. I think we have generally handed over our responsibility. 'The televangelist will preach the message. I don't preach the message.' But we're all called to do it.

"So if that can become a key thought, that my Christianity means I share my faith with everyone around me, no matter what the means, I think that needs to be addressed. Internet evangelism shouldn't be seen in isolation. It needs to be part of a bigger picture and a bigger strategy."

NetCaster Tony Whittaker believes social networking is an ideal way to evangelize online. "Many Web sites, on almost every subject you can think of, offer blogs, bulletin/message boards, or e-mail discussion lists where you can build relationships with others. YahooAnswers is a ready-made opportunity too (http://answers.yahoo.com). Build relationships within your own areas of interest."

Twitter and Microblogging

The latest phenomenon to flood the Internet is Twitter, a Web site and service that allows users to send short text messages—up to 140 characters in length—from their cell phones or computers to a group of people. Twitter was launched in 2006 and quickly gained popularity. It was designed as a quick and easy way to keep friends and colleagues informed about one's daily activities.

But very soon Twitter started being used by celebrities, politicians, ministries, and other companies as a way of telling their followers what's new. Twitter messages—also known as "tweets"—are only distributed to people who have elected to become followers. Messages can also be sent via instant messaging, the Twitter Web site, or a third-party Twitter application.

You can connect Twitter to your Facebook or MySpace account so that they can be updated when you "tweet."

Twitter allows for "mobile blogging," which is the process of updating a blog from a cell phone or other digital device, and immediately sends the updates to followers. This allows a person, company, or ministry to have what is called a "microblog." A microblog contains brief entries about the daily activities of that individual or company to keep friends, customers, or colleagues up-to-date.

Small images may be included in a microblog, along with short audio and video clips. Several Web services like Twitter exist, including some that send text messages to several people at once. Other microsites use a concept similar to Twitter but combine the microblogging facilities with file sharing or other features. Other microblog sites provide similar options inside a closed network used by corporations, ministries, nonprofits, or universities.

In April 2009, Hollywood actor Ashton Kutcher beat out CNN to become first to have more than a million followers on Twitter. "We now live in an age in media that a single voice can have as much power and relevance on the Web, that is, as an entire media network," Kutcher said on *Larry King Live*. Kutcher also acknowledged that while he was able to get so many followers because he is well known, he was trying to show that anyone can have a voice and let their story be told.

"I think it's really important that Twitter is not about celebrities. It's not a platform for celebrities," he said. "In all these interviews and things, it's been celebrity—you know, people who have been on TV. It's really about everyday people having a voice. And I don't want it to be dwarfed by celebrity."

The same week Oprah Winfrey sent her first "tweet" to the seventy-five thousand people who had signed up to follow her. "HI TWITTERS. THANK YOU FOR A WARM WELCOME. FEELING REALLY 21st CENTURY." By the end of that day, her followers were more than one hundred thousand.

Caroline McCarthy, who writes a CNET News blog about social media, told CNN, "The power of Twitter is about the millions of people using it and how easily it is to filter and aggregate their thoughts and conversations."[3]

Dave Winer pioneered the development of blogs, syndication (RSS), podcasting, and Web content management software. He describes the advantages of Twitter on his Web site, Scripting.com:

1. It's a network of users, with one kind of relationship: following. I can follow you, and you can follow me. Or I can follow you and you

don't follow me. Or you can follow me, and I don't follow you. Or neither of us follow each other. Pretty simple. Just arrows at either or both ends of the line, or no line at all.

2. It's a micro-blogging system. Posts are limited to 140 characters. Enough for a bit of text and a link. This is a powerful idea, but not a new one. If you read Scripting News before February of this year, it was partially a micro-blogging system. When it started in April 1997, it was all micro-blogging. The earliest Web sites, from TBL, NCSA, and Netscape were also micro-blogging systems.

3. A relatively open identity system. I've said it before, Twitter or something like it, could be the holy grail of open identity. . . . Twitter, with it's ultra-thin user interface, and light feature set, and simple API (more on that in a bit) and the nothing-to-lose attitude of its management, may be the breakthrough. Or it could be Facebook, with its much larger user base and a management that also likes to roll the dice. The key is lots of users, a growing user base, and an API with no dead-ends.

4. An ecosystem. . . . Compare it to Apple, who reserves for itself and a few partners, under terms we don't know, the right to develop rich apps for the iPhone. Twitter takes the traditional PC industry approach, give everyone equal power, make it a level playing field and let the chips fall where they may. This means that if the people at Twitter miss an opportunity, the rest of us have a shot at providing it for ourselves and others.

So what do all these parts add up to? Users and relationships between users, their ideas, and an ecosystem. It's probably the basis for some pretty hot apps. Will it be possible to monetize them? Without a doubt. People who say that Twitter hasn't figured out how to make money don't understand the role technology companies play in the much larger media and communication ecosystem. Ideas gestate here, grow up, find users, and then find customers.[4]

Web evangelist Tony Whittaker suggests these possible uses for Twitter in ministry: Apart from using it to network with friends and colleagues, there may be fruitful ways to use it more interactively in ministry. It seems unlikely to develop as a direct evangelistic tool, but rather one that builds and maintains existing relationships. Here are some possible directions to consider:

- In local TV—using it to receive questions from viewers.
- Sharing ongoing reaction to a shared event with friends. For example, a group of friends could arrange to Twitter their thoughts during a TV film or show. A group of students watching, for example, a set film relating to their course, could also interact in real time. This could be an opportunity to share any spiritual parallels they notice.
- It also works when people are in the same geographic location. For instance, attendees at a large seminar or meeting can Twitter their questions to the speaker, which has the advantage that other participants can view the questions (unlike when attendees send questions by text message or e-mail).
- For instant response help from friends, Twitter is useful. As well as urgent prayer requests, here is an example from a Christian geography teacher:

> "The best tweet I sent ever was about six months ago I had to teach a geography cover lesson and Twitter-requested some pointers to water cycle animations on the Internet, just a couple before the lesson. I got two responses before it started and the best most helpful actually during the lesson!
>
> Who to follow, and who to block (if they follow you). I adopted a range of strategies as I worked out how the network worked. Early on I 'followed' people who followed people who were evidently leaders. Now I tend to be interested if the other tweet is either a teacher or involved in Christian ministry, but like real life there are exceptions."

So Twitter is yet another potential lure in the tackle box for the NetCaster to use to point people to a relationship with Jesus Christ.

Social Network Danger Zones

Social networks can be a great tool to do Internet evangelism because they provide a way for people to start a conversation. Unfortunately, what people say can be offensive and in some cases pretty shocking. Before beginning a ministry outreach through a social network like Second Life or MySpace, the NetCaster must first prayerfully consider the dangers involved. If the person is a new believer or has a particular weakness to certain sins, he may fall into temptations that are rampant on these sites.

"It's not just a matter of who is able to get on the Internet," John Sorensen cautions, "but who is able to get on the Internet and not fall into temptation. If a person has not dealt with that, then he shouldn't get into Second Life.

"I took my son into Second Life and went to Calvary Chapel and started looking around. Then I visited buildings around it and that was the only day that I participated. The 'Red Light District' is everywhere in Second Life. There is open pornography everywhere you look."

Safety Tips for Social Networks

While social networks offer tremendous opportunities for evangelism and ministry, they also can be very dangerous if not used properly. The Internet is the world's biggest information exchange. Anyone can potentially see the information you post online, including employers (or potential employers), teachers, the police, and complete strangers, some of whom could be dangerous.

By providing information about yourself through blogs, chat rooms, e-mail, or instant messaging, you can communicate, either within a limited community or with the entire world. Social networking sites give you the ability to connect with people—but you want to avoid connecting with the wrong people.

Don't post information about yourself online that you don't want the whole world to know. While social networks can increase your circle of friends, they also can increase your exposure to people who have less-than-friendly motives.

Sadly, there are numerous stories of people who were stalked by someone they met online, who had their identity stolen, had their computer hacked, and worse. One tragic story demonstrates the potential dangers of sharing information on the Internet. In the late 1990s, a troubled young man named Liam Youens began stalking a fellow classmate, Amy Boyer. For several years he was obsessed with her from afar and online. She had no idea she was being stalked. Youens created a Web site dedicated to Boyer, chronicling his daily obsession about her.[5]

On October 15, 1999, Youens drove to Boyer's workplace and fatally shot her as she left work. He then committed suicide.

The U.S. Federal Trade Commission has created a Web site with social networking safety tips: http://www.ftc.gov/bcp/edu/pubs/consumer/tech/tec14.shtm. TechMission also has a Web site called www.SafeFamilies.org with more suggested safety tips for using social networks.

The Bible encourages us to be wise as serpents and harmless as doves. The NetCaster who wins souls through social networks is wise, but be sure to learn and follow basic online safety advice before you venture into this exciting ministry field.

Chapter Seven

Becoming a Master Caster:
How Do You Attract the Fish?

I went to Google and typed in 'Is there a God?' When I got to your site and saw the list of articles, it freaked me out. Every single question I had, it was all right there. I read through the whole site, even the articles for guys and the one about eating disorders. I read about how to become a Christian. When I read that God doesn't care about the specific words, He cares about our hearts, it was so freeing. So I just prayed, 'Yeah, what it says on the screen, God, I want that; I want to know You.'"

This testimony from EveryStudent.com is a wonderful example of how someone who had questions about life, eternity, God, Jesus, faith, and religion was able to find eternal life as a result of a Google search online.

Here's another one:

> I just typed in "WHO IS GOD" into Google and got your Web site. I really hope you can answer some of my questions, because I feel very lost at the moment.

These days the Web is almost anything you want it to be. But people will be attracted to your site only if you offer something that scratches their itch. The key is to find out what people want and then position yourself to provide it—and with it the gospel message. There are some key concepts to help the NetCaster work to make his or her site stand out from the millions of Web sites online—including the bridge strategy, search engine optimization, and the marketing funnel.

Using the Bridge Strategy

Many Christian Web sites make the assumption that their audience wants a religious experience online. But most effective NetCasters are careful to first build trust with a seeker, fostering a relationship through conversations, and then gently leading the person from the place of seeking to the place of surrender to Christ.

The wise NetCaster will do this by a subtle approach. All cross-cultural missionaries understand the importance of building cultural and communication bridges. This is just as true with online evangelism. Tony Whittaker calls this process of connecting with seekers the "bridge strategy."

As I have already pointed out, the vast majority of Christian sites are created for believers using "Christian-eze" language, jargon, and assumptions. Most non-Christians are not able to relate to these sites, even if they do find such pages. But most people are searching online for what interests them—news, entertainment, sports, health, sex and relationships, advice on personal problems, hobbies, local information, humor, music, movies, celebrities, and countless other things.

"It's important to understand that the Web is a 'pull' medium, unlike literature and radio, which are linear 'push' mediums," explains Whittaker. "Generally speaking, people go online to search for information. The pages that relate to the subject of their search pull them in. Most people are not searching for Christian material, and so of course, will never find it. If they do by chance come across an obviously Christian page on a search engine listing when looking for a secular subject, they're unlikely to click on it. If they do, they probably will not stay."

If there is no pull drawing seekers to a site, they will most likely never stumble upon that Web page. So evangelistic Web sites are often designed to meet the felt needs of seekers, pulling them toward the answers they're searching for. This strategy requires a great deal of intensive research and observation to determine the needs of a targeted audience, and then a large amount of creativity and work to design a site with all the elements necessary to attract seekers.

"The conventional Web site, which combines bridge strategy pages with a nonpreachy and appropriate presentation of the gospel, remains the most important type of online outreach," says Whittaker. "Writing yet another presentation of the way of salvation is not going to reach many of them, unless we 'fish on the other side of the boat,' by using the bridge strategy."

Whittaker suggests that NetCasters create Web pages on secular subjects or felt needs to target specific groups of people. Bridge pages must be written with integrity and they must be contextualized so they relate to their targeted readers. There are several ways you can draw people across the bridge to pages explaining the gospel:

- Your testimony: Whatever sort of site you have, make a link to "Meet the Webmaster" or "My Story." Here is a chance to share your testimony. (But don't call it "testimony"—that's Christian jargon.) Introduce yourself first, where you live, what you like, etc. Then go on to explain how something happened that changed your whole view of life.
- "Meaning of Life" links: On any type of Web site, you can offer a link such as "What is the meaning of life?" or "Finding real fulfillment." These do not sound preachy or even Christian, yet show some sort of nonthreatening "spirituality" content. As well as leading to a sensitive explanation of the gospel, they also offer the opportunity to provide FAQ-type apologetics answers.
- Parable meanings: Jesus used stories with a message as His main means of evangelistic communication. And He didn't always explain the meaning—He left people to let them think!

"This does not mean that we make trick pages that are not really about the subject they claim to be," Whittaker cautions. "If we write a page about restoring VW cars or breeding mice or a favorite musician, the page must truly be *about* that subject. It must be as good and informative as possible, maybe with many helpful links to other pages on the subject."

A "bridge" page should not *look* Christian in its language or design. The more mainstream a Web site appears the better it will communicate with those with no Christian background. "It may make little mention of Christianity at all, allowing the links to other pages to progressively offer more material on the gospel. It's important to get the balance right."[1]

Fish Finder: Search Engine Optimization Strategy

The NetCaster who will embrace the bridge strategy as part of their ministry goal will reap the rewards of that effort. And through a proper understanding of marketing techniques and search engine optimization, those rewards can be even further multiplied.

A vital and necessary method of attracting people to your evangelism site is to employ search engine optimization (SEO), which is designing a Web site so that search engines can easily find the pages and index them. The goal is to have your page appear in the top search results through Google, Yahoo, or other search engines. Optimization includes the choice of words used in the text paragraphs and the placement of those words on the page, both visible and hidden inside meta tags, which are key words to help search engines find your content.[2]

Search engine optimization increases the volume of traffic to your Web site from search engines through the use of targeted keywords. SEO includes working within your site's coding, presentation, and structure to coordinate keywords and concepts so they will be recognized by search engine "spiders" (links throughout the Internet that grab content from sites and add it to search engine indexes).

In the process of search engine optimization, research must be conducted to determine the most strategic keywords. This involves finding the relevant keywords, determining their popularity, considering the competition, and deciding how the keywords can be used within the content. An excellent resource to learn more about search engine optimization is http://www.seobook.com/blog.

Australian-born John Edmiston is a missionary Bible teacher who has been in full-time ministry using computers since 1991. He believes it's imperative for the Internet evangelist to be knowledgeable in the science of search engine optimization. It begins with becoming specific in targeting your audience.

"My most specific pages—one on theophostic counseling, one on cloning, one on breaking curses—are the ones that get the most visitors. So if you want to reach a tribal culture and you want to do it evangelistically, you ought to have a Web site on how Jesus can deliver you from witches, curses, and spells. You use all those terms—'Sanguma man,' 'curses'—very specific terms that are going to be relatively rare in Google. They're just specific to that culture."

"You have to think of how specific you can make it. You've got to think about your end user typing in a search engine—and then that search engine taking them to your page. You have to keep this process in mind always.

"How is God going to send you that seeker? You can come up with a very specific article that will be the only thing on the Internet on that topic. And once you've done that, you ask, 'What sort of person is going to this unique Web site? What are their spiritual needs? How do they respond?' You create these unique pages. Then those unique pages are your harvesting tools."

Edmiston explains that a page about God, a page about salvation, or a page about the Bible is probably going to have no hits at all, unless you spend a lot of money on Google ads. But if you don't have a lot of money for Google ads, you need to make your pages, articles, and videos specific. "The key to success in any communication strategy is thinking deeply about simple things. A lot of people say don't bother with keywords anymore. I disagree heartily. I think keywords and end tags are just totally necessary. I was at a conference last year where someone was saying you didn't need to worry about SEO. But he was getting less hits than my worst Web site."

Edmiston gives these practical hints for building your SEO:

- Search engines mainly read HTML. Some search engines are starting to read PDFs, but they're not as good as HTML. (I keep going back to HTML because that's what gets you the hits.) You can create something in Word, then go to Dreamweaver and clean up the HTML. Then the search engines will pick it up.
- You will have few hits during the first three months. It takes awhile for the search engines to notice. Most search engines won't find you for six weeks.
- The oldest pages get the most hits because they're deep down in Google. Each Web site builds an audience over time, as it's linked to other Web sites. If you add database-driven Web sites, you offer something that other people can link to.
- Be careful when you're changing your pages; keep up with the old URLs so you don't lose those links. Never change your URLs. You must allow things to build up.
- Offer specific targeted responses to currently hot topics. Keep up with political events, scientific events, or new movies that are coming out.

Another effective search engine optimization (SEO) tactic is maintaining a significant amount of text on your Web site to attract the spiders. Tiffany Maleshefski of SEO Tools explains the concept. "The code to text ratio represents the percentage of actual text in a Web page. Our content ratio tool extracts the text from paragraphs and the anchor text from HTML code and calculates the content ratio based on this information.

"Why is the code to text ratio important for SEO? The code to text ratio of a page is used by search engines and spiders to calculate the relevancy of a Web page. A higher code to text ratio gives you a better chance of getting a good page ranking for your page. Not all search engines are using the code to text ratio in their index algorithm, but most of them do. So having a higher code to text ratio than your competitors gives you a good start for on-site optimization."[3]

"Search engines can sometimes be technical," says CBN.com Marketing Director, Alex Demeshkin, "but the basic principle behind it is to write as if you were writing for humans, using their language, and the language that they would use if they were researching a topic. Then the chances are the search engines will pick it up.

"With CBN.com, for example, I look, periodically, on what search queries people use when they come to our Web site. Often one of the most popular searches is homosexuality and Christianity or divorce and faith—things like that. Clearly someone is struggling with an issue. Something is going on and it drives them to go and search for information specifically on that topic, on that issue. By virtue of being well optimized for search engines, with our resources on our Web site, hopefully we can help someone to receive help from the Lord on their problems."

Buying Google Ad Words

Another approach is to buy ad words on a search engine like Google. Alan Beeber of Campus Crusade shared "that there are a variety of traditional as well as digital marketing options that ministers can be used to share the gospel. Which ones are chosen depend on the message, medium, desired results, target audience, budget, ect.

"The other thing is, because the Internet is the place where people do their private thinking and searching, people are going to use a search engine. So obviously you want to be optimizing one's site for search engines."[4]

It's important to understand, however, that search engine optimization is not some sort of magic wand that will attract people to your Web site. SEO is not necessarily an appropriate strategy for every circumstance. Other Internet marketing strategies can be equally as effective, depending on your vision. Effective marketing may include a combination of:

- Search engine optimization using research and keyword placement;
- Links from other Web sites and blogs;
- Paid advertising on search engines and other pages;
- Designing high-quality Web pages to engage and persuade;
- Keeping on top of technical issues that may keep search engines from crawling and indexing your Web site;
- Constructing analytical programs to enable you to measure traffic and improve your conversion rate.

One of the most important things you can do is test, test, test— employ a Web analytics software system like Webtrends or Omniture and find someone to analyze the data and work with your content team to meet the needs of your audience.

Funneling the Fish

Along with a thorough understanding of search engine optimization, another important element of Internet evangelism is marketing. Web evangelist Richard Helsby explains the concept of the marketing funnel and Internet evangelism.

"There's a lot of work out there from marketers and Web designers to help you make your site as effective as possible for a return on investment. It's all about trying to move the person from the initial page to take an action that leads them toward the marketing funnel. They're trying to get you to the shopping cart, and then they're trying to get you to check it out.

"They are also trying to get your information so they can contact you and connect with you. And they'll offer things on the Web site for free. Sometimes they'll offer information and you have to sign up with your e-mail address. There is a lot of marketing best practices and some of that can be applicable to Web evangelism.

"If I want to encourage a person to explore Christianity further and connect with my community and this process, what can I use? Do I offer them something? You don't want to turn it into a business. But you can think of the principles that work. You can ask how you can get their e-mail so they can start corresponding. Or you can start sending newsletters about faith and something like that."

These same marketing techniques and principles can work for Internet evangelism. You can build an evangelistic Web site, but is anyone going to find it? The same approach that people would use to advertise their Web site online, you can use to promote your evangelistic Web site, from search engine optimizing to actual paid ads.

CBN Digital Media Marketing Director Alex Demeshkin expands on the marketing funnel concept and how that might be used in Internet evangelism. "In the commercial world, there are two types of marketing. There is the 'branding' concept, where it's not like we don't want to sell online, but it's not really about finishing the sale at this very moment. We want to build value and promote our brand. The second type is 'direct marketing,' which says, 'OK, what can I do to get the sale as quickly as possible? And how can I streamline the efficiencies of all the processes?'

"You could argue that a similar concept could be used on the Web in Internet evangelism. You start with the question, 'How do I advertise?' You first start with branding. You may not necessarily get a person to believe, pray, and invite the Lord into their hearts online—it may or may not happen. Chances are it won't happen online when you are in a chat room with a person, or something like that. But branding Christianity is an effective way to communicate what Christians are about—the love of God. It's a powerful communication channel, and a brand advertising channel. As Christians we can certainly use the Internet for that.

"Second, in certain cases, perhaps you do have a chance to have some sort of conversion. The person might not be a believer now. But you can invite them by communicating with them and asking them to visit your Bible study group. You do some sort of groundwork, and then later, down the road, they become a Christian.

"These are measurable things. So if you've chatted with somebody online and you've convinced them to try to hook up with a local Christian fellowship somewhere where they are, that's a trackable conversion, so to speak. Or if you got them to use a church finder and you got them to come to church on a Sunday morning; if you prayed with them and got them to agree, or you get them to post a prayer request, to a degree that is measurable.

"I have said many times, the Internet is just a tool. You have real-time technologies like chatting, instant messaging, Web cams, and all sorts of things that I utilize in the commercial world. So if you come to a Web site and you're browsing on a product page for a while, and a window pops up that says, 'Do you need help? Can I help you with something?' there is a real-life person there. Now, they may be chatting simultaneously with fifty other people. So it's not like they're helping only you. But it's an Internet technology, and you need to look at what you're trying to accomplish."

Demeshkin recommends that the NetCaster examine the role that they want the Web site or the medium to play in the overall strategy.

"Maybe you're helping to plant a church somewhere. You can use the Internet to communicate more effectively. Yahoo! Groups has a discussion board where people who belong to a certain religion, agnostics, or people who don't believe anything come together and ask each other questions. The premise is to find out how a person representing one or another religion would answer a certain question. It could be a worldview question, or merely a simple question. These are examples of building relationships and connection, getting to know people and using the Internet as an evangelism tool."

By employing these "fish finder" techniques, you may have varying results. The key is to try something, test it, analyze the results, and then decide if it's bearing fruit. If it is, keep doing it. If not, try something else. But the point is to keep trying, and trust God to lead you into fruitful fields.

Chapter Eight

A New Day in the Marina: NetCasters and the Local Church

Heather was an average, thirty-year-old woman struggling to find her purpose in life. She would flip-flop all over the place, searching for the one thing that would bring her the joy she so desperately craved.

She had a career and owned a home and a car. She had two wonderful children and lived in a good neighborhood. But something was missing, something she couldn't put her finger on. But she knew that it wasn't there and that it should be.

After looking for satisfaction in relationships, in her career, and in the party scene, she finally decided she should try to find a church. She went a few times but never found one that felt like home.

An online acquaintance from the business world, Lisa, sent Heather an e-mail announcing that she was becoming a biblical coach and was looking for guinea pigs. Because she loved to learn, and she thought it wouldn't hurt, Heather signed up.

Lisa asked Heather to complete a questionnaire, requesting that she be honest. So she was. Heather cringed sending in the questionnaire, but

Lisa's response was only that the two were a lot alike. They began chatting online via instant message. Heather soon opened up about some of the things going on in her life. One day as they were chatting, Heather started to cry.

She admitted that recently when a pastor spoke at her son's basketball game, she felt compelled to talk to him about God but didn't. The next thing she knew, Lisa was giving her the telephone number to the church where her son played ball. She instructed Heather to call and make an appointment to talk to the pastor.

Lisa wasn't taking no for an answer and so Heather called. Heather talked to the pastor for nearly two hours in his office. She told him that she thought it was particularly cool that a pastor had a MySpace page.

After the visit with the pastor, Lisa gave Heather some Bible verses to read and told her to journal at least three pages every day. Heather did what she said and then e-mailed Lisa with her questions.

The pastor invited Heather to visit the church on Sunday. After talking to Lisa at length, Heather told her that she would go.

Saturday rolled around, and her friends were all going out—downtown . . . to a bar. Heather decided she would join them. She told Lisa before she went that she was going to go to church the next day. Then she told everyone at the bar that she was going to church the next day.

When Heather finally rolled in the door at 5 a.m., drunker than a skunk, she determined that there was no way she was going to church. She didn't set the alarm. In her drunken stupor, she figured that if she was up in time, she would go; and if she didn't get up, then the church would be there next week.

But at 8:00 a.m. Heather was wide awake. She tried every bed in the house and the couch, trying to get back to sleep. She was tired and hungover and wanted to sleep.

By 9:00 a.m. Heather got up and contemplated going to church. But the reality was that she didn't want to go. She was afraid. Heather tried to talk herself out of going to the church, but she didn't want to tell Lisa that she didn't attend. Heather had promised she would go.

She went to the church and found that it did things much differently from the church she attended when she was a child. The church had a projector, lively music, and people praying and crying. Heather cried too.

She took notes during the sermon. She had questions like, "How come it was OK for David to kill Goliath when the Bible says 'thou shall not kill'?" She wrote them all down on her bulletin so that she could ask Lisa.

When she got home, Heather sent Lisa an instant message telling her that she had been to church. When Lisa asked her about the night before, she told her all the details, including being wide awake at 8:00 a.m. after being out all night.

What Lisa said next amazed her. She told Heather that she prayed for a wake-up call so she would get to church!

For two weeks Heather and Lisa went back and forth on saying a prayer of salvation. Heather struggled because it was so different from what she knew. But Lisa was very patient. She never yelled at Heather or gave up on her.

For Heather, those two weeks were horrible. She did nothing but cry, read the Bible, and pray. But she just wasn't going to say the prayer of salvation. She was stubborn.

One night Heather couldn't take it anymore. "I felt like I was having an arm-wrestling match with God and I gave in," Heather explained. "I said that prayer. And then I told Lisa. And then I e-mailed the pastor."

This is what she wrote:

> So MySpace isn't the avenue that I would normally pick for this, but I'm on my laptop and not with my address book. At least I know where to find you.
>
> We talked two weeks ago. In the time since, I have read more of the Bible than I ever have in my life. I've been to church; I've journaled; I've prayed. Man, have I prayed. I've attended Bible studies and prayer groups. I've been working on righting wrongs.
>
> But also in this time I have felt more out of sorts than I have in a long time. I cry at the drop of a hat.

I cry for no reason. Why do I feel that I am lost and alone?

Well, I think I figured all this out . . . and it has to do with that prayer. I think I've been hesitant because I don't fully understand. I was raised differently in that this "saved" thing isn't the norm for me.

Now Lisa says it's a spiritual struggle and that God is working on me. Great! I need work, but I *can't* keep going on like this. I feel like God and I are having this arm-twisting game and I'm ready to say, "Mercy!"

So here goes . . . I said that prayer. I sat here in my bed, tears in my eyes, and decided that I had nothing to lose. I know two things. I can't go on by myself anymore. And I want a relationship with Jesus. I want what you all have.

On February 15, 2007, Heather became a Christian. Her life hasn't been the same since.

More than a year later Heather posted a message on Lisa's blog, thanking her for her online ministry. "Oh, how grateful I am for the Internet, and for you, and for your witnessing to me so that I could have the life that I have now, and in turn, share Jesus with others."

NetCasters and the Local Church

The local church is a key part of God's plan for making disciples and fulfilling the Great Commission. These are the ground troops—pastors, cell group leaders, youth leaders, young adult leaders, homeschoolers, Christian school teachers, street evangelists, music ministers, children's ministers—the list goes on and on.

NetCasters—people who share Christ on the Internet—are part of the air forces, which include bloggers, people with affinity sites, people who work on chat and message board forums, television ministries, radio ministries, and so on.

As Heather's story demonstrates, the air forces need to work with the ground troops, and the ground troops need the air forces to see the gospel of the kingdom preached to all peoples. We need each other. As the apostle Paul wrote, "So the eye cannot say to the hand, 'I don't need you!'" (1 Cor. 12:21).

In order for the Great Commission to be fulfilled, all the various forces in God's army must be coordinated and cooperating to strategically take the gospel to those who need to hear.

The time for NetCasters to arise and work with the local church to win the lost and then equip them as disciples is now. The need couldn't be more critical.

As I've already pointed out (see chapter 1), researcher George Barna indicates that within this decade, as many as fifty million people might rely solely on the Internet to provide all of their faith-based experiences.[1] This activity will include virtually every dimension of the faith community, such as online church services, chat, message board forums, video, devotionals, streaming video sermons, virtual meetings, broadcasts to those who are homebound, theological training—the list of possibilities for using digital technology to preach the Good News is only limited to our Spirit-directed creativity.

Equipping the Local Church—Ephesians 4

Writing to the believers in Ephesus, the apostle Paul explained how the structure of the church was to work most efficiently and effectively.

> "And He personally gave some to be apostles, some
> prophets, some evangelists, some pastors and teachers,
> for the training of the saints in the work of ministry."
> (Ephes. 4:11–12)

The apostles, prophets, evangelists, pastors, and teachers are to equip *the saints* for the work of the ministry—each individual believer must be empowered to do his or her part. The Great Commission can never be fulfilled as long as the ministry is only being done by the full-time, vocational ministers. Paul was pointing out that it is the role of every disciple, or saint, to do the work of the ministry. Every Christian has a calling to fulfill in this life.

The wonderful thing about the Internet is that once the language barriers are overcome, it becomes possible for any believer to reach one-fourth of the world's population from a laptop on their dining room table! And now with mobile digital devices in the hands of more than three billion people worldwide, and more soon to come, any NetCaster is potentially connected with half of the people living on planet Earth!

What an amazing time to be alive and be serving Jesus.

Discover, Develop, Deploy

Church consultant Sandy Kulkin speaks of the "three Ds" of discipleship—*discover* your calling and spiritual gifts, *develop* these things, and then *deploy* into that ministry.[2] Obedience to the call of God on your life is the issue. Discovering, developing, and then being deployed into that ministry is a lifelong adventure in which you must maintain an intimate relationship with God through prayer, Bible reading, and fellowship with other believers.

"I think the very first thing would be to take Mary's advice," says NetCaster and professional writer Rusty Wright. "Mary, the mother of Jesus, in John chapter 2, verse 5, told the servants at the wedding of Cana, 'Whatever he tells you to do, do it.'

"A real key is asking God, 'Lord, what do You want me to do? Do You want me involved in this?' And if He does, you had better not be caught dead anyplace else. If He doesn't, you don't want to be involved in it.

"A second thing would be to do everything you can to learn how a non-Christian thinks and feels." Wright has resources at www.rusty wright.com with text and video explaining, "How to Think like a Non-Christian Thinks."

"A third thing I would ask God is to break your heart with the love for the lost, so that you would maybe even literally weep over the plight of people who will spend eternity without Christ. Ask God to give you a burden and zeal to do everything you can to try to reach them."

Wright also recommends that NetCasters get training in how to communicate with non-Christians in a way that catches their attention and doesn't push them away with overly religious language. TruthMedia, an outreach of Campus Crusade in Canada, has great training programs in online evangelism through writing articles and chat room ministry."

Fishing Lessons: Training the NetCasters

So what does a person with a passion for evangelism and a desire to start NetCasting on the Web need to get started? John Edmiston has developed a series of online evangelism training courses through Cybermissions.org.

"I'd ask them first who their friends are, and who they relate to. A person might come to Christ and he might be a mad hockey fan. Do you know any Christian guys in hockey who can give their testimony? You can be passionate about hockey and be passionate about Christ. So you get hockey testimonies and analogies to hockey that relate to Jesus.

"There's something you have an affinity with, and do something that's specific," Edmiston explains. "Start small and cheap. Do something like 1and1.com for Web hosting. Set aside two thousand dollars. I know that sounds like a lot—but if you're starting a ministry, that's not a lot of money. That'll give you the domain names and allow you to buy the software like Dreamweaver that you'll need to do the job properly. Get the right software and make sure you know how to do what you're doing."

Edmiston recommends that NetCasters think strategically about the first two seconds when people are looking at your Web site, your video, or your podcast. The attention span on the Web is very short. If that first two, three, or four seconds aren't good, people are clicking away.

"You've got to hook them in the first few seconds, and hold the type of people you want in those first few seconds. So if you're doing a video, and the first few frames are boring, boring, boring, they're gone. It's similar with a Web page. If it takes too long to load, they're gone. You've got to make the first paragraph interesting—so you've got to be a journalist.

"Most of the stuff I work on, I want to lead someone to Christ in five minutes. I often use the Romans Road, or approaches like that because by the time I've gotten to that page, they're already asking, 'How do I become a Christian?' If they've clicked on the link to go to that page, they are ready. So just give them the gospel—don't mess around. Keep it simple. Give them short sound bites. Get them to the player in under five minutes."

Then follow-up materials can be a lot longer, because once seekers have made a commitment, they really need to read. But even the follow-up messages are only one page each. Keep it simple. Keep it tight.

"I don't mind getting politically involved," Edmiston explains, "but I separate that drastically from Internet evangelism. It's a different arena. You have to ask yourself:

- Will this become dated?
- Will this offend?
- Will this bore the person?
- Is my testimony relevant to the whole group of people I'm seeking to reach?

"When you're doing evangelism, you have to have the testimony that fits your audience. So it's imperative that you know the demographics of your intended audience and you continually aim at these people."

Internet evangelism has great potential, and the response rate online is extremely high because you have an audience that has selected to learn about Jesus. Edmiston explains that his online response rate is the same percentage that Billy Graham has for a major crusade. "So online, I'm as effective as Billy Graham—because they're preselected. It's 2 percent—that's what Billy Graham gets. If he's preaching to fifty thousand people, one thousand people come down front. If I share the gospel with fifty thousand people online, one thousand people make a decision."

Edmiston is reaching nearly a million people a year through his various Web sites. This is an amazing achievement for one person, and he is quick to point out, "But I've been doing it for years, and I have some volunteers who are really key."

Edmiston offers three levels of Internet evangelism training on Cybermissions.org—beginner, intermediate, and advanced. Here are other sources for NetCaster training:

- Internet Evangelism Network Online Training: http://www.webevangelism.com/otoe/index.php
- Internet Evangelism Day Training: http://www.internetevangelismday.com/training-videos.php
- TruthMedia Training: http://training.truthmedia.com/training_video

Dissing Church, but Into God

As people continue to interact with each other online, increasingly they are turning to the Internet to find answers about God, the Bible, religion, and spirituality in general. The new connectivity to the Internet in cities around the world couldn't have come at a more strategic moment in history. In the new millennium, people are moving from the countryside into the wired megacities like never before.

Surveys tell us that they are also hungry for God like never before:

- Web pages dealing with God, religion, and churches grew 1,429 percent between 1999 and 2004.[3]
- A 2003 Gallup poll indicates that a vast majority of Americans say religion has an impact on every area of their life.[4]
- The online faithful are somewhat more active as Internet users: On a typical day, 63 percent are online; 56 percent have been online for six years or longer; 60 percent are broadband users.[5]

According to the 2006 survey on Americans' religious beliefs "American Piety in the 21st Century," published by Baylor University, 82 percent of Americans are Christians; 90 percent believe in God; nearly three-fourths, 71.5 percent, pray regularly; and almost half, 49.2 percent, attend church at least once a month.

According to the Baylor study, nearly half of Americans (47.2 percent) identify themselves as "Bible-believing." Americans are demographically as religious and as Christian, as they ever have been, but they are far less likely to be loyal to a particular denomination. As a whole, Americans are drifting toward more informal forms of evangelical Christianity.[6]

So while Americans seek God, they are leaving traditional church. According to a 2007 survey by LifeWay Research, seven of ten Protestants in America, ages eighteen to thirty, both evangelical and mainstream, who regularly attended church in high school, say they quit attending by the time they were twenty-three years of age.

In most cases the decision to leave was not planned far in advance. Only 20 percent of these "church dropouts" agree that while they were attending church regularly in high school, they "planned on taking a break from church once [they] finished high school." Many of those who drop out do eventually return. Among church dropouts who are now ages twenty-three to thirty, 35 percent currently attend church twice a month or more. Another 30 percent attend church more sporadically. Thus, about two-thirds of those who leave do return at some level.[7]

According to Rainer Research, 70 percent of those that leave the church do so between the ages of eighteen and twenty-two. Of these eighteen- to twenty-two-year olds who drop out of church, 51 percent describe the church as "judgmental." Only 39 percent of those who dropped out of church saw their churches as "caring." Forty-one percent said their churches were "insincere." Only 20 percent described their churches as "inspirational," 30 percent said their churches were "authentic," and 36 percent called their churches "welcoming."[8]

For many who leave the local church, the Web has become their source of information about God and religion. So for the Internet minister the concern should be in connecting with people online where they are, not where we think they should be. NetCasters should see Internet ministry as a means to connect with the lost in a forum where they are comfortable sharing their innermost thoughts.

We should always encourage people to find a local church where they can grow in relationship with God and fellowship with other believers. But we must also be gentle and sensitive to those who have been wounded in the past.

Some of the people who will come to Christ on the Internet may have no problem making the transition to becoming a part of a local church. But others may have been wounded by other Christians, may have poor teaching on the importance of the local church, or may feel uncomfortable in public settings, and it may take some discipling to convince them to become a part of a local church. The Internet is a wonderful safety net for people like this who need to have their wounds healed so that they can once again become a part of a face-to-face body of believers.

Local Church NetCasting

I often get blank stares from pastors when I speak to them about getting their people involved in Internet evangelism. "That is the World Wide Web, and we're interested in the local scene," some declare.

I tell them two things. First, the church whose light shines farthest, shines brightest at home. And second, there are plenty of ways to evangelize your local community through the Internet. Often communication through the local church has been one-directional. Today, through user-generated content and community features, online communities are gathering in the local church and beyond to encourage discipleship and evangelism.

More and more, local churches are developing innovative, creative, and informative Web sites that are both serving as digital meeting places for discipleship within the body of believers while also drawing in seekers. Many youth groups and young adult ministries have linked from their church Web site to a MySpace or Facebook page for their particular group. Using the tools and applications in these social networks, and others like them, they feature forums and chat rooms so people can interact with others from church throughout the week, rather than only through face-to-face encounters within the church building.

Ways local churches can use the Internet include:

- Post videos of services on the church's Web site and on other video outlets.
- Report to members what's happening through the week in and through the church.
- Post audio sermons online and offer them as podcasts.
- Post short-run, creative video.
- Post teaching series in in-depth online Bible studies with video, audio, and text podcast.
- Skype meetings for staff and volunteers who can't be at the physical location—or if they don't want to meet face-to-face.
- Facebook, MySpace, and other social networks for chat and message boards.
- Post local church video logs and calendars.
- Create a local community event portal with links back to your church and to a gospel presentation.
- Create a local services page with information on various church, community, educational, and governmental services for people in need.
- Create a local Christian online dating service.
- Create a forum for online interaction for shut-ins, people traveling, or prisoners with Internet access.

Through a church, you can use Skype, Facebook, Tangle, or other networks to promote and advertise what the church is doing. You don't need a $1,000 dollar camera—all you have to have is the vision and the training to do it.

Local Churches and Worldwide Missions

The Internet provides a new and exciting way for people with a vision for reaching the nations for Christ to do so without leaving their local community. Churches can create Internet evangelism teams, trained within the church, to go online through various forums and volunteer agencies to witness to the lost—both in your local community and around the world. Churches can provide computer labs and weekly meeting times for the NetCasters to gather, pray together, share testimonies and words of encouragement, and then go online to win the lost.

Ministries like Campus Crusade's Global Media Outreach (GMO), TruthMedia, and NeedHim.com recruit volunteers and provide them with e-mail addresses of people who are seeking. Using e-mail as a key part of its response strategy, Global Media Outreach is recording more than 3,800 decisions for Christ worldwide through the Internet per day.

The GMO system is designed around a virtual e-mail base. Volunteers never use their real e-mail addresses because security is important. "It's all browser-dependent using virtual e-mail. And you correspond with the person back and forth. It's a threaded conversation. So if they come back, they come back to you," explains Alan Beeber, director of Global Media Outreach for Campus Crusade for Christ.

If an issue arises that a volunteer doesn't feel comfortable dealing with, the volunteer can reassign the entire thread to somebody else. "Let's say it's a marriage problem," Beeber gives as an example. "The volunteer says, 'I don't know how to deal with this.' Well, we're a group, so we can send that to someone else if need be. If it's suicide, abortion, or difficult questions, or it's a language we can't figure out—we have parts of the system that can take care of that very well."

Beeber says it's easy for volunteers to sign up and get started. They can decide how many daily e-mails they can handle. The community leader can read the threads and determine if a new volunteer is theologically sound or not. If a local church would like to start an Internet evangelism outreach, this would be a great way, he recommends.

"A good example is a Baptist church in Arizona that had a donor who had previously supported Crusade and some of its major ministries. I talked with him and he said, 'OK, I'll give this a try. I'd really like to make Jesus more of an issue at Easter.' So he created a Web site, www.jesusandeaster.com."

"The evangelism director at his church became the community leader. We were able to redirect any contacts originating from any of our sites back to Arizona. If they came from Arizona, we'd send them back to this community."

Beeber received an e-mail a few weeks after the four-week campaign. This donor wrote, "Alan, I have never seen anything this effective in my life. We had 301.7 indicated decisions for Christ every day. I will be back."

The contacts can come from someone locally or from anywhere in the world. "We're able to say, 'How many people do you want to expose to the gospel?' We can literally give you a good idea of how many you'll expose, how many will respond, how many e-mails you'll get."

Dr. Sterling Huston of the Digital Evangelism Network believes there is great potential for churches to use the Internet to touch both their local community and the world. "It's wonderful that you're trying to reach your communities right here and now, and we hope that you will be able to do that even more effectively in the days ahead. You can enhance that by using the Web and making it known to people in your neighborhood or in your city that there is a Web presence they can go to and find out about the gospel, about your church, about the things they offer for Christians to do in that way.

"But I would go further than that to say that probably most churches in some way support some sort of home or foreign missions. That's very important that they do that. But that is a very expensive way to send the gospel out to other parts of the world. Whereas you can have a reach through the Web that can be kept contemporary, can be done very economically, and can touch not just one geographic spot in one part of the world, but can touch the entire world that maybe speaks the language in which you are conveying this.

"So here is a marvelous tool that can extend their mission outreach and multiply their exposure many times over. It allows a whole new generation in their congregation who love to use the Internet to participate in evangelism."

Now is the time for pastors of local churches to catch the vision of ministry through the Internet. As churches launch various Web outreaches and remain consistent, Internet ministry often explodes with new growth. And fruit recruits. Once your church members start bearing fruit, other people will want to be a part of it.

Chapter Nine

The Fishing Village: Who's Catching Them?

Around the world thousands of heroic NetCasters give of themselves every day to share the happy news that God is love and He cares for people so much that He created a worldwide network of computers so that they could hear that Good News!

One of the wonderful things about working on the Internet is that I have had the pleasure to meet many of these heroic NetCasters, both in real life and in online! I'd like to introduce a sampling of them to you, knowing that these few represent thousands just like them who sacrifice their time and energy to make Jesus real to seekers in the electronic forum we call the Internet.

Tony Whittaker: Internet Evangelism Day

Some people have a profound affect on the world around them just by being who they are. That's the way I feel about my dear friend Tony Whittaker, whom you've already gotten to know in the pages of this book. So instead of introducing you to the coordinator of the Internet Evangelism Day and the editor of the Web Evangelism Bulletin and the Digital Evangelism Issues blog (www.internationalevangelismday. com/blog), I'll just let you be a fly on the wall, so to speak, in one of our conversations.

von Buseck: How can local churches encourage their people to become involved in Internet evangelism?

Whittaker:

- Take time to discuss how digital media has transformed all communication, both offline and online, and give us a key way to share the good news.
- Consider presenting this potential to the church, using Internet Evangelism Day's downloads: PowerPoint, video clips, music, drama, and handouts.
- Help church members (including the youth group) who are wondering if their gifts could be used online. Consider appointing a coordinator or enabler to help them do this. Opportunities include social networking on Facebook, etc., making short videos for YouTube, gaming and Second Life, blogging and Twitter, Web site creation, and offering to be an e-mentor for inquirers on large outreach ministry sites.[1]
- Discuss ways of making the church Web site "outsider friendly."

von Buseck: What are your goals or desires for the Internet Evangelism Day?

Whittaker: To help the global church understand, and decide to use, the digital media for outreach. And to demonstrate different strategies that are working, right across the board, from outreach sites to Twitter, and to illustrate them with positive stories from both Web evangelism practitioners and those who find Christ online.

von Buseck: What are some mistakes beginners make when doing Internet evangelism?

Whittaker: Probably several: (1) Not understanding their target readers and their needs. Or, indeed, not even consciously having a target reader at all, just a vague assumption of "everyone." (2) Using our "default mode" of communication—i.e., speaking to, or as if to, other Christians. (3) Using all sorts of Christian jargon and assumptions.

von Buseck: Groups like NeedHim are integrating IE into their overall ministry strategy. Do you see this as an effective use of the Internet for ministry?

Whittaker: Definitely. The Web is not just another communication method, but a hyper-medium that subsumes, delivers, and interconnects all other media: text, MP3, video, audio, TV, letter writting, shopping, tracts, mobile phones, games, everything! Above all, it is a relationship builder. NeedHim's integration of TV ads with Web, SMS, phone, and e-mail is an example of the sort of integration we need across the board. Web evangelists are seeing this potential—for instance in several areas of the world, there are informal networks of outreach people: Web, radio, satellite, TV, Bible correspondence courses, outreach teams on the ground, and local churches. By working together, they are creating far more effective ways of helping inquirers, discipling converts, and integrating them into local churches.

- http://www.internetevangelismday.com
- http://www.web-evangelism.com

TruthMedia (Campus Crusade Canada)—Karen Schenk

Through a network of Web sites that reach out to many segments of society, TruthMedia ministers directly to hundreds of thousands of people every month. It's team of staff and volunteers is passionate about using technology to share the gospel of Christ by creating online communities of evangelism and discipleship. The emphasis is on connecting seekers in need with committed people who can help them.

TruthMedia Director Karen Schenk manages the editorial and interactive teams and oversees a corps of more than four hundred volunteers. "One of my favorite changed-life stories was when I had the opportunity to lead a woman to the Lord and then discovered she only lived a mile from my home. Since that time four years ago, her husband

and two children have come to know the Lord and are now serving in our local church.

"Another encouraging story was about a gentleman who wrote us on a Saturday morning, saying he had planned that weekend to take his life as he was a terrible husband and father. I e-mailed him that Saturday morning and asked him to wait until we could get him some help. We then had one of our online counselors speak with him and help him through some very difficult months. He recently e-mailed our site (two years later) to let us know he is walking with the Lord and doing very well.

"It's an incredible privilege to participate in a ministry that reaches thousands for Christ. It's exciting to see people volunteer and have significant ministry impact from their homes and businesses in their areas of interest and in conjunction with their schedules. The Internet is a great place to minister!"

- http://truthmedia.com/index.php
- http://powertochange.com

Top Chretien—France

One of the most successful Internet evangelism sites in the world is Top Chretien led by Eric Celerier in France. One of the Top C NetCasters, Nathalie, shares her story of how God is using her to take the gospel to the world without ever leaving her home in Paris.

"While I was living in Paris, my heart burned for people around the world, living their lives without knowing Jesus. As I was reading stories of missionaries, I felt called to become a missionary myself. One day, after an evening service, the soft and loving voice of the Lord whispered to me through the voice of my pastor, 'You don't have to go abroad to be a missionary because all the nations are in Paris.'

"Eight years after that evening service, I am now involved in Internet evangelism and work in full-time ministry. Through the Internet, I have been able to see thousands of decisions for Jesus every minute from all over the world. Our Internet evangelism tool is Knowing God (www.godrev.jesus.net/joy-in-heaven). It exists in seven languages. Our vision is to develop the Web site into twenty-eight languages in order to reach two hundred fifty million visitors by the year 2020.

"My responsibility on the team is to supervise the 103 counselors in France, who follow up on those needing help or asking questions about faith and God. I encourage and serve these faithful men and women who give a large part of their time to counseling. I even follow up on inquirers myself. Up to now, I have mainly been involved in one-to-one contact. Even though I am not very skilled on the computer—that is to say, not so technically talented—I enjoy sharing online or reading many encouraging testimonies.

"It's worth it, Lord, to stay in France and see one life at a time touched and changed."

- http://www.topchretien.jesus.net
- http://godrev.jesus.net

David Bruce: Hollywood Jesus

In 1997 Billy Graham challenged Christians to use the Internet for good. David Bruce took the challenge seriously, even though he had never been on the Internet. With a background in media (NBC), pastoring (MDiv), and being a missionary at heart, he went to the nearest Barnes & Noble where he picked up books on Web site graphics and design.

"With cross-cultural missiologist Don Richardson's *Eternity in Their Hearts* serving as inspiration, I set to work creating a vehicle whereby I could use the culture to win the culture. Thus, Hollywood Jesus was born.

"The idea behind the site was simple: to mine the movies for redemptive analogies, to find bridges in popular culture for the presentation of the gospel. The method, or a version of it, is tried and true. The apostle Paul used this cultural-engagement approach to reach those who had gathered on Mars Hill in Athens."

The result is HollywoodJesus.com, a Web site geared to exploring "pop culture from a spiritual point of view." Since its launch in February 1998, the site has received more than six hundred million visits. It averages a million visitors a month.

"The goal of the site is to share Christ, and I am happy to report that I correspond with about a hundred people at any given time via e-mail about their journey toward our Savior. The site started out as something I did part time and has evolved into a full-time ministry. It has opened many wonderful opportunities to share Christ—including on Fox News, *Time* magazine, the *New York Times*, ABC News, etc. It has been an amazing 'Go ye into all the world' experience."

* http://hollywoodjesus.com

Christy Talbert: NetCaster

Christy began her evangelistic ministry on the Internet when her son, Josh, was a toddler. She often found herself home at night without much to do and began chatting on America Online. Soon people began coming to Christ while in chat with Christy. She became convinced that online chat was a powerful witnessing tool. Several years later Youth for Christ approached Christy about building a team of Internet evangelists.

This team, named YFC Online, has evolved to encompass several evangelistic venues. TeenSpaceColumbus.com is a MySpace-type web community developed to give local teens a safer place to congregate online. Through TeenSpaceColumbus.com, kids enjoy making new friends as they build relationships with committed adult Christians who share their faith when the opportunity arises.

In addition to TeenSpaceColumbus.com, Christy works closely with Groundwire.net. There she serves as a spiritual coach and volunteer consultant regarding online ministry. She is currently exploring Second Life as a potential new ministry site for Youth for Christ and has already seen several salvations through the Second Life ministry.

Hundreds of people have made decisions for Christ through YFC Online and Christy's chat ministry over the past fifteen years. These individuals range in age from nine to senior citizens. They live all over the world and have diverse spiritual backgrounds. Thousands more have received encouragement, counsel, a sympathetic ear, and prayer in times of need.

- E-mail: SunburyBuckeye@gmail.com
- Second Life: Christy Justice

Sean Dunn: Groundwire (Youth For Christ)

Champion Ministries and Groundwire (GW) started in 1995, and are based in Castle Rock, Colorado. They conduct an outreach program that reaches people all over the world. The organization is the product of Sean and Mary Dunn's vision to reach young people with the incredible gospel message that allows them to have a personal relationship with their Creator.

Groundwire is working to reach every student in the world through effective and creative communication of God's Word, His love, and His purpose for each of them. By placing sixty-second Christ-centered spots on secular and Christian stations all over the world, they are working to flood the culture with pictures of authentic faith, attractive Christianity, and a loving God.

In addition to helping kids meet their spiritual needs, Groundwire volunteer support coaches have contact with those dealing with heaven and hell issues. Groundwire currently is broadcasting the message of Christ with more than twelve million people on a weekly basis on both secular and Christian radio. This encompasses more than 1,200 radio stations on five continents.

"We are reaching those who are not seeking a spiritual voice," says founder Sean Dunn. "From the prodigal to the struggling Christian to the total unbeliever, we are planting seeds and seeing the harvest."

- http://www.groundwire.net

Drew Dickens: NeedHim Ministries

Since 1997, NeedHim has received more than 800,000 calls and presented the gospel to more than seventy thousand people. The NeedHim radio spots are heard on more than twelve hundred radio and television stations, and the 888-NeedHim is displayed in countless print formats. Each year the www.NeedHim.org Web site receives four million visits, and volunteers respond to more than ten thousand emails and twelve thousand instant message chats about Christ from all over the world!

NeedHim works together with Luis Palau, American Tract Society, Hope for the Heart, Jesus Video, Campus Crusade for Christ, Ron Hutchcraft Ministries, National Day of Prayer, Moody Broadcasting, and others.

Drew Dickens, president of NeedHim, explains that depending on how users Google it, NeedHim is on thousands of Web sites. "It's fun. This is very viral.

"All volunteers are trained to do phone, e-mail, and chat. All volunteers start monitoring a chat or a phone call. Most of them start by replying to an e-mail. Then they move toward either phone or chat."

In a culture that prizes anonymity, NeedHim offers a place for people to find answers without confrontation. NeedHim is not a prayer line or a counseling center; it is an evangelism center, "to intentionally present the gospel."

- www.NeedHim.com
- http://needhim.org

John Edmiston: Australia and United States

Dr. John Edmiston directs a missions agency called Cybermissions that trains people in Internet evangelism to contact unreached people groups through Internet cafés and Web sites. He has been ministering online since 1991. He is also an adjunct professor at Fuller Seminary, teaching evangelism and cybermissions.

"I first got involved when I had a 2,400-baud modem and a computer without a hard drive back in 1991. I was involved in a lot of discussion groups with cults. I did apologetics with cult groups and also a lot of the online debates in the early bulletin boards and chat rooms.

"Then in 1994, I went absolutely full time in Internet evangelism, and I have been full time ever since. In 1994, I started the prayer page, which was one of the first Christian Web sites on the new Internet. This was a Web site that allowed people to post prayer points. Then I set up one of the first Christian dating sites on the Internet. But it quickly got overwhelmed and I had to shut it down."

Edmiston developed the Asian Internet Bible Institute after he saw a need for many of these pastors, particularly in areas where there is a mixture of Muslim and Christian, to have support in their missionary work. He started setting up Internet cafés to support the pastors with donated, recycled computers.

"At the moment I'm running Cybermissions.org, and I'm also running the Asian Internet Bible Institute site. http://www.globalchristians.org/articles/ is the online seminary. Cybermissions.org is training Internet evangelists.

James Watkins: Writer/NetCaster

The slogan of NetCaster and author James Watkins is "heavy topics with a light touch." Watkins employs that light touch as he writes, speaks at conferences, and interacts with people through his Web sites. He travels throughout North America and overseas, ministering with humor, drama, and practical messages to communicate with teens, parents, adults, pastors, and writers. As an author, he's written thirteen books and sold more than two thousand articles, devotions, editorials, hard-news stories, poems, reviews, scripts, short stories, and song lyrics, as well as more than one hundred photos.

Connecting with people was what first interested Watkins in the concept of evangelism on the Web. "The potential audience caught my imagination. It's a way to reach millions of people with virtually no expense. Your Internet service provider monthly fee—that's about it. As far as good stewardship, it's a great way to evangelize."

"As a writer, I'm always looking for an audience. When I first heard about the World Wide Web in 1995, I thought, *What an opportunity to getting your work out there.* I went online for the first time in April of 1997.

"If you're not on the Web, you don't exist. Paul would be at ApostlePaul.com. I know he would."

- www.jameswatkins.com

Ship of Fools—U.K.

Ship of Fools was launched on April Fools' Day 1998 and quickly grew into an online community as well as a webzine, a magazine for the Internet. "We're here for people who prefer their religion disorganized," says the Ship's editor and designer Simon Jenkins. "Our aim is to help Christians be self-critical and honest about the failings of Christianity, as we believe honesty can only strengthen faith."

Regular features include the Mystery Worshipper, the Caption Competition, and Gadgets for God. Ship of Fools has also run a number of projects, including The Ark, an online game show, and Church of Fools, an early experiment in online 3-D church.

The Laugh Judgment, their investigation into funny and offensive religious jokes, prompted journalist Julie Burchill to say: "If one must choose a modern symbol of what is so good about Britain, I would choose Ship of Fools."

Alongside these is a thriving online community, including the famed Heaven, Hell and Purgatory bulletin boards, in which shipmates debate everything from "Religion and Buffy the Vampire Slayer" to "The Status of Mormonism" to "Hitchcock and Catholic Guilt."

Ship of Fools coeditor is Stephen Goddard, who met Simon Jenkins at theological college in London in the late seventies. "As committed Christians ourselves, we can't help laughing at the crazy things that go wrong with the church, and we're also drawn to those questions which take us beyond easy believing. In the end, we want to make sense of the Christian faith in today's complex world."

Fully independent, iconoclastic, and debunking but also committed to the ultimate value of faith, Ship of Fools attracts visitors more interested in searching questions than simplistic answers.

- http://www.shipoffools.com

EveryStudent.com—U.S.

More than a Web site, EveryStudent.com is a strategy allowing campus ministry to actually reach other students, whether on a campus or in an entire country. It is a way to bring the gospel to young people, to train and equip Christians in evangelism, and to release students to build movements using the Internet.

Since EveryStudent.com started in 2000, the strategy has seen dramatic annual growth. There are now EveryStudent.com sites in more than twenty languages that collectively reached more than six million people during 2007, resulting in 110,000 new believers. Campus directors around the world are excited about the possibilities of growing their ministries and developing student-led movements of multiplication through the site. Young people report that EveryStudent.com is a safe place for students to explore who God is and what it's like to know God.

One student wrote, "Hi, my name is April and I had e-mailed you a few months ago and asked you some questions. I just wanted you to know that I asked Christ into my life two weeks ago so I am now your new sister in Christ. Thanks for taking the time to answer my questions. It really meant a lot that you took the time to e-mail me when you did not even know me."

The site is made up of persuasive, evangelistic messages on topics that university students care about. EveryStudent.com also gives students an opportunity to e-mail someone a question and receive a personal e-mail reply.

Typically, 1 to 2 percent of all visitors indicate decisions to receive Christ while on the site.

- http://www.everystudent.com

Rusty Wright: Writer/NetCaster

"I'm no techie! How could I ever use the Internet to reach people for Christ?" NetCaster Rusty Wright asks. "I'm no techie either," he confesses. "I know how to send e-mail and read the news online, but that's about it. My own interests involve communication, especially relating Christ to secular audiences." But over the years, Wright has written numerous evangelistic articles to help reach nonbelievers, in print and on more than three hundred Web sites around the world.

Wright explains how he first got involved in Internet evangelism. "Several years ago, a couple of friends involved in Internet ministry, Keith Seabourn and Allan Beeber, asked me to send them all my articles so they could put them online. I didn't understand what all that meant, but they said it would make the articles available free to people around the globe. That seemed like a good thing. Keith's Web site, Leadership University, aimed to collect thousands of articles supporting the validity of Christian faith. Allan's Evangelism Toolbox became an online 'Yellow Pages' (directory) of evangelism resources. They helped introduce me to Internet outreach."

At a convention in Amsterdam around the same time, he saw a brochure that said, "The Great Commission Is Going Digital; Are You Ready?" That piqued his interest. "Maybe God wanted me to focus my energies on Internet evangelism," he thought.

"The simplicity and pervasive nature of the Internet was allowing people to find and use these articles in ways I had never imagined. I could sit with my laptop in my office, on an airplane, or in a hotel room and compose an article that would tactfully nudge people toward Christ or biblical principles. Then, by pushing a button, I could send it to Internet publishers who would make it available to people around the globe.

"This seemed almost too good to be true. What a potential for spreading the Good News!" His articles now appear in several languages: English, Spanish, Albanian, Croatian, Hungarian, Italian, and Polish. "People just kept translating and posting them. It seemed beyond my control or ability. God gets the glory for this.

"Internet evangelism offers you a dazzling array of possibilities to communicate Christ."

- E-mail: RustyWright@aol.com
- www.rustywright.com
- http://www.leaderu.com

Walt Wilson, Allan Beeber: Global Media Outreach (Campus Crusade for Christ)

Global Media Outreach is recording more than thirty-eight hundred decisions for Christ per day—with 1.3 million salvations online in 2007. This ministry of Campus Crusade for Christ supports more than forty different Web sites that reach specific, targeted people groups around the world. Trained staff and volunteers lead people to Christ, answer e-mail questions, and do online mentoring and discipleship.

"The good thing is that we literally can record the number of people who are clicking yes on our form," explains Allan Beeber of Campus Crusade. "So the software and the strategy is rapidly scalable. That was one of the things we really needed because we estimate that if one person can take five or ten e-mails a day—which wouldn't take long to answer—if you do the math in terms of how many people we need to expose to the gospel, our goal is to have fifty thousand online volunteers, or as we sometimes call them 'online missionaries,' by the year 2020.

"A good example would be Student Venture, a very effective high school ministry of Campus Crusade for Christ. In fact, it is the most effective in terms of field staff and decisions on the field. We put up two sites for them. One of them is www.meant4more.com. That site in one year recorded seventy-five hundred indicated decisions for Christ. And that is as much as they saw from all their staff. The ramifications of what I'm saying are huge for Christian missions.

"Internet ministry is not something that is a supplanting ministry. It is a strong addition to ministry. You need both boots on the ground, and you need an air force. And so Internet ministry provides that air force.

"Let's take meantformore.com. People can come to that site because a Student Venture staff member was handing out business cards on a college campus. They may do a blitz on the campus, or just off the campus, and they'll have these simple little cards (http://meantformore. com/home.html). We also have one for our flagship site, http://www. whoisjesus-really.com/main.htm.

"Or we use Google advertising. Students may type in 'purpose of life' in Google, and they'll see the site on the front page. If you search for 'Jesus' in Yahoo, our site is number one, which is by the grace of God. Also if they type in some of the search terms that we use, they'll come to a sponsored link and they can click on that."

To become a Global Media Outreach volunteer go to:

- www.globalmediaoutreach.com
- http://www.globalmediaoutreach.com/get_involved/volunteer.html

More NetCaster Heroes

This is merely a small list of the thousands of NetCasters around the world who are giving their time and treasure that others may know freedom in Jesus Christ. They are all heroes!

- Way of the Master with Ray Comfort and Kirk Cameron: http://www.wayofthemaster.com
- Dare2Share: http://www.dare2share.org
- Probe Ministries: http://www.probe.org
- Leadership University (Keith Seabourn): http://www. leaderu.com/menus/apologetics.html
- Strategic Digital Outreach (Frank Johnson): http://www. strategicdigitaloutreach.com
- To the Next Level (Doug Reese): http://www.tothenext level.org
- Off The Map (Jim Henderson): http://offthemap.com
- Doug Yeo of the Boston Symphony Orchestra: http://www. yeodoug.com

- Life Without Limbs (Nick Vujicic): http://www.lifewithoutlimbs.org
- Ephesians 6:10 Ministry (Lee J. Bloch): http://www.e610.com
- InterVarsity, Questioning Faith: http://www.ivpress.com/questioningfaith/resources
- VisionSynergy (Dave Hackett): http://www.davidhackett.com and http://www.visionsynergy.net
- Your Destiny, Your Choice (Bill and Wilma Watson): http://www.ydyc.org/index.php
- Evangelism Toolbox (Allan Beeber, Campus Crusade for Christ): www.evangelismtoolbox.com
- Simply His Blogger (Lisa Boyd): http://www.simplyhisblogger.com
- Not Religion: http://www.notreligion.com
- Ron Hutchcraft: http://www.hutchcraft.com
- Student Venture (Campus Crusade): www.meant4more.com
- Think Christian: www.thinkchristian.net
- Look to Jesus: http://www.looktojesus.com
- Movie Glimpse: www.MovieGlimpse.com
- ExWitch Ministries: http://exwitch.org
- Ancient Crossroads: http://www.ancientcrossroads.org
- All About God (Greg Outlaw): http://allaboutgod.com
- Desperately Seeking Sanity (Heather's Blog): http://www.desperatelyseekingsanity.com
- Rob Williams: http://orangejack.com
- Proverbs 31 Ministries (Laurie Webster): http://www.proverbs31.org
- The Internet Mission (Matt Rich): http://www.theinternetmission.com
- Brandywine Community Church (Greg Lipps): http://www.brandywinechurch.org
- Holy Mama Blog (Kelsey Kilgore): http://holymama.typepad.com

- CalCast (YWAM): http://www.podomatic.com/tag/calcast
- LifeChurch.TV: http://www.lifechurch.tv
- Flamingo Road Church: http://www.flamingoroadchurch.com/main and http://www.troygramling.com
- Jesus-Online (Germany): http://www.jesus-online.de

You can join this list of NetCaster heroes. Contact me at www.vonbuseck.com to learn more!

Chapter Ten

NetCaster Networking

"If we are together nothing is impossible. If we are divided all will fail."—Winston Churchill

The great British statesman was paraphrasing the biblical themes of unity and cooperation when he called the free peoples of the world to rally against tyranny in his day. As believers, we must rally together against the tyranny of sin and worldly deception that holds so many in ignorance and bondage.

It is imperative to have NetCasters networking.

In this chapter I want to supply a starting point for connecting and partnerships among ministries and individual NetCasters. As a member of the Internet Evangelism Network executive committee, I have the privilege of meeting on an ongoing basis with other Web ministers. I am always amazed and encouraged by the innovation, creativity, strategies, and dedication of these wonderful men and women of God.

Here are some of the ways a ministry or an individual NetCaster can find partnerships and collaboration with other Internet evangelists.

Internet Evangelism Network

The purpose of the Internet Evangelism Network (IEN) is to stimulate and accelerate Web evangelism within the worldwide body of Christ. The focus is on collaboration—linking partners together in this mission to reach our world with the Good News of Jesus Christ—http://www.webevangelism.com.

The goals of the IEN are:

- Promote Internet Evangelism: Inspiring strategic thinking and resource development to empower the church for Internet evangelism and initial follow-up.
- Facilitate Collaboration: Encouraging collaborative efforts and connecting partners and resources for Internet evangelism.

Members of the Internet Evangelism Network provide support through financial donations and in-kind contributions and are involved in the IEN e-newsletter, IEN annual meeting, and the development of new tools and resources for Internet evangelism.

IEN members are at the forefront of new initiatives designed to connect those involved in Internet evangelism. IEN members connect with individuals, organizations, ministries, and churches that have a passion for sharing the gospel online.

I sat down with IEN Chairman Dr. Sterling Huston to talk about the IEN history and goals.

von Buseck: Tell me how the Internet Evangelism Network was birthed?

Huston: Back in 1995, I said to Bob Coleman, who headed up the evangelism institute at the Billy Graham Center, that we really ought to do a consultation on using the Internet for evangelism. It was just beginning to emerge, and the Web was being made available to the public. Bob took this vision and began to organize this consultation under the auspices of the Billy Graham Center. Their first goal was to have CEOs and people at the executive level of leadership from major organizations to come with the goal of fifty. They ended up having to shut it off at one hundred people. They held a three-day consultation in April 1997 at a local hotel.

The outcome was not only the great interest of people showing up to be a part of that, but also a consensus that there ought to be some kind of a continuing body to further enhance and facilitate collaboration among ministries toward this goal of Internet evangelism.

The consultant who worked with the original group said he had never seen a group come together as quickly with a sense of a goal and a vision as he saw here. I believe this was because it was about evangelism, and because these were people who had a passion for that. We can unite around evangelism much quicker than almost anything else.

It was also intended to be not an organization but a guided collaboration that helped to facilitate the passion people had and assist them with information, resources, and networking.

Out of that original mandate, then, a small group of us met among the planning committee and began to shape a body that would include some practitioners, some providers, as well as a good cross-section of parachurch and church leaders to start a committee that we would come to call the Internet Evangelism Network.

It was started with the idea that we would have the minimum amount of organization needed in order to accomplish our goals and our purposes. That particular body has evolved over time. Usually the service providers, because they appear in some way to have a vested interest, eventually left the committee but still were networked with it. It has ended up being, at this point, primarily people who represented transdenominational ministries or parachurch ministries, and some major denominational representation.

We finally decided that the IEN should be primarily a stimulant and a catalyst for bringing people together, networking, communicating, and providing resources for organizations and ministries that wanted to use the 'Net for evangelism purposes.

von Buseck: What are some of the things you'd like to see happen through the IEN in the coming years?

Huston: The mission of the IEN, simply stated, is to stimulate and accelerate global evangelism using the Internet. I would like to see us continue to be a catalyst to bring people together who have resources to commit to this. By that, I mean resources of programs and ideas and technology and, obviously, dollars to support that. And as much as possible, create product and create a kind of knowledge base that we can give away to both the church and parachurch.

I would like to see the IEN be a place of coordination, whereby ministries that are springing up all over the world can have some place that they can not only receive information that helps them but also share information that helps others.

There needs to be some kind of clearinghouse where we can help people on the other side of the world, "We've already tested this. It already works, or it doesn't work." I would like to see it be a place that has an intentional focus on communicating again, and again, and again that the Web and digital technology are the new media frontier. We must be utilizing these.

We need to see evangelism as more than only inside the church. We need to see it as a way to have access to a whole world of people who live in this media form and expand our outreach enormously by doing that.

von Buseck: You spoke of the IEN using these words: catalyst, convener, connector, commender, consultant, communicator, and a credible voice. I counted them and there are seven—so through the IEN a NetCaster could sail the seven Cs! (laughter).

Huston: Well, I'd like to pick up on the credible voice. If anything, because some significant organizations have gathered around the table and have said "We need to collaborate because the mission is bigger than any one of our parts. We trust one another, and we can help one another get this job done." I think that provides a statement to the public at large, as well as an endorsement to the Christian community that will help the cause of using the Net for evangelism and for sharing our faith."

The Internet Evangelism Day

One of the ways that the Internet Evangelism Network is promoting Web outreach is by cosponsoring the Internet Evangelism Day. This special annual NetCasting event serves as a resource for churches, Bible colleges, and other groups to promote Web evangelism.

The purpose of the day is to:

- increase awareness of the Internet as a powerful evangelistic medium;
- encourage, enable, and envision churches, other Christian groups, and individual Christians to use the Web for outreach;
- offer specific strategies and training for Christians in this area.

The Internet Evangelism Day is held on the last Sunday of April each year and promoted extensively through the Internet and other media outlets. To learn more about this exciting opportunity to promote Web outreach go to http://www.internetevangelismday.com.

This site offers a myriad of downloadable resources with suggestions and background material to help your church or group create an effective IE Day focus. The materials enable you to create a mix-and-match, do-it-yourself program. The promotional program can be five minutes or fifty, and it can be included within a church service, after-church meeting, midweek home group, Bible college seminar, or any other appropriate meeting for Christians.

On the IE Day Web site you can follow the "planning" link in the left-hand menu bar to view and download these resources. There is also a seventeen-slide PowerPoint presentation if you need to explain the concept to your leadership or decision-making team.

GUIDE Network (Global Use of Internet and Digital Evangelism)

Another group that encourages collaboration and cooperation among NetCasters is the Global Use of Internet and Digital Evangelism (GUIDE) Network. GUIDE is an informal networking resource, linked with Internet Evangelism Day and Web Evangelism Guide, Digital

Evangelism Network, Global Christian Internet Alliance, Lausanne and visionSynergy.

The GUIDE network gathers to enhance the global spread of the gospel in multiple languages via the Internet and mobile digital devices by networking with practitioners to:

- share resources and information;
- encourage Kingdom collaboration;
- help the body of Christ to embrace and engage in Internet/ mobile evangelism.

Dave Hackett of VisionSynergy founded the GUIDE Network to help ministries collaborate and cooperate and avoid duplicating ministry efforts. "I worked first with the IEN and got acquainted with it," Hackett remembers. "Then I stumbled upon the inaugural meeting of the Muslim Internet evangelism group and was brought right onto the steering committee. The effort that came out of that was a long drive, almost two years, to form a global cross-language, cross-organizational Internet evangelism network.

"We saw quickly that if there was a Muslim one, and that has an exciting degree of specificity, and there is the North American one here—this English-speaking IEN, and there are some possible strands of hope for Chinese, Korean, Spanish, and so on that might separate off and form. We'll need some mechanism and way of pulling those together so we can share what we're learning. Or the opposite, we can seed and help start more specific ones."

Hackett points out that currently there is neither a Hindu or Buddhist Internet evangelism group. "I mean, China, Buddhism, and Internet—does anyone see things clicking here?

"In Japan there is 100 percent Internet penetration. We've been going crazy trying to spark mobile evangelism through Alpha Japan, OMF, and JEMA (Japanese Evangelical Missionary Association). We're sending out the seminal pieces to help them to understand the dynamics and to consider it. And that's another way we work, to help them catch a vision."

Many of the GUIDE Network partners are involved in the cross-cultural missions community as well as the new media, with a unique web of relationships to draw on. The network includes a Yahoo! Group (which has merged with the IEN GlobalForum group) and a range of other resources, including a wiki and blog on mobile evangelism, a group for those interested in children's online outreach, and free articles—both evangelistic and evangelism-challenge for Christians.

GUIDE Network aims to draw together those interested in web evangelism and mobile device evangelism, with a particular emphasis on the huge opportunities in the non-Western world, in languages other than English, and to the unreached peoples world.

Patrick Johnstone of Operation World writes of GUIDE Network, "I am delighted to see the networking of Christians concerned for using the Internet for outreach. We all have much to learn to make best use of this medium. May the GUIDE Network be a key tool in equipping many Christians to become effective Internet evangelists and disciplers."

Here are some recent additions for the GUIDE Network:

- GUIDE Network Yahoo! Group (http://www.tech.groups. yahoo.com/group/guide-network): This is a place to network with others, share news, and ask questions on any aspect of Web/mobile evangelism. You may wish to opt for a daily digest, to restrict the number of e-mails you receive.
- Mobile Evangelism Wiki (http://mobilev.pb.com): Wiki, listing the ways Christians are using the mobile platform in outreach and discipleship.
- Tracking Mobile Ministry Blog (http://davehackett.blogspot. com): A resource page about mobile device evangelism.
- Children's Web and Digital Media Ministry Network (http://community.godrev.com/group/ childrenswebanddigitalmediaministrynetwork): A place for networking, sharing vision, ideas, resource, and strategy for reaching and teaching children through the Internet and digital media. You will need to join GodRev; you can then

ensure that your settings will send only e-mails in relation to this group.

* Lausanne's newsletters Connecting Point (http://www.lausanne.org/lausanne-connecting-point) and Lausanne World Pulse (http://www.lausanneworldpulse.com).

VisionSynergy

VisionSynergy is a small team with much experience in creating viable and enduring mission networks and mission partnerships between churches, agencies, and organizations to advance global evangelization, especially among unreached people groups. The ministry hosts a networking resource site (www.powerofconnecting.net) that includes their book *Well Connected* (www.connectedbook.net) by Phill Butler.

VisionSynergy believes that an international Internet evangelism network will significantly increase the growth and effectiveness of existing and new online evangelism efforts. It works to connect experts around the world to help Christian groups network together to fulfill the Great Commission.

VisionSynergy has identified at least six such opportunities with high-impact potential for world evangelization. In each of these sectors, strategic networks can share best practices, case histories, and resource information; help fill gaps and reduce overlap; and provide encouragement and hope.

1. Evangelism among the 2.5 billion illiterate people who are the last frontier of the unreached.
2. Evangelism in the nearly 400 2/3rds world cities of more than 1 million inhabitants each in and around the 10/40 window.
3. Evangelism of more than 1 billion Internet users in languages other than English.
4. Economic sustainability of the emerging, persecuted church in Islamic, Hindu, Buddhist, and animist settings so these churches can support their own church growth and evangelism.

5. Linkage of the extensive North American resources among laity, local churches, mission agencies, Kingdom funders, and denominations that share a commitment to reaching the unreached.

6. A growing global company of individuals working to encourage kingdom collaboration, networks, and partnerships but who lack information, resources, training options, and connection with each other.

More information can be found at VisionSynergy's Web site, http://www.visionsynergy.net.

Regional Expressions May Develop

Dave Hackett of VisionSynergy believes that a key way that global Internet evangelism network might develop is through the linking of regional or language-specific networks. Early collaborative efforts are already under way:

- Several ministries are preparing an online evangelism effort for French speakers (http://www.connaitredieu.com). There are more than twenty-seven million French-speakers online.
- Ministries are using the Web to reach out to Farsi speakers (http://www.kelisatv.com).
- Numerous seeker-friendly, evangelistic Web sites for the Islamic community are operating (http://thelightoftruth.com), containing both English and Arabic versions.
- China appears ripe for online evangelism with an Internet population of 103 million, second only to the United States. Nearly half of Web users in China are under the age of twenty-four.

John Edmiston of Cybermissions.org refers to a "tunnel and blast" strategy of using the Internet to tunnel into a culture to find a "person of peace," then building a relationship and equipping the person to win the community and thus blast the gospel. In the developing world one person may be directly or indirectly connected to three hundred people.

Edmiston views global Internet evangelism as part of God's unfolding purpose. "God has planned the use of Internet evangelism from long ago and stretched out His hand to bless it. We are at a critical period of world harvest when much needs to be done and yet many countries are closed to conventional means of preaching the gospel. God has raised up Internet evangelism and cybermissions as one way of meeting this need and is powerfully blessing it and making it effective."

Global Christian Internet Alliance (GCIA)

The Global Christian Internet Alliance is an international network of Christian ministries using the Internet to help fulfill the Great Commission. GCIA's mission is to provide convenient access to quality Christian Internet resources in all the major languages of the world.

The Global Christian Internet Alliance grew out of an international gathering convened by Christianity Today International in May 2001. Participants included ministries representing eight major languages: Chinese, Dutch, English (U.K. and USA), German, Japanese, Korean, Portuguese (Brazil), and Spanish (Chile). Most were leading Christian publishers or broadcasters seeking effective ways to extend their evangelism and discipleship ministries through the Internet.

Following this first conference in Chicago, alliance partners developed an international channel on their own sites with multilingual links to other affiliates. Since then, conferences have been hosted by GCIA partners around the world: Amsterdam (2002), Toronto (2003), Paris (2005), Seoul (2006), Berlin (2007), and San Antonio (2008).

The conference program focuses on practical case studies with partner ministries sharing strategies and methodologies in their areas of expertise and strength.

This growing network now includes twenty-four ministries representing fourteen major languages: Arabic, Chinese, Dutch, English (Australia, Canada, India, South Africa, U.K., USA), French, German, Italian, Japanese, Korean, Norwegian, Portuguese, Russian, Spanish

(Chile and Costa Rica), and Swedish. Together these languages represent more than 85 percent of Internet users, and new partners are being added to the alliance as more languages get connected to the World Wide Web.

Partnership in the Global Christian Internet Alliance is by invitation only. To contact the GCIA, send an e-mail to GCIA@christianitytoday.com, or visit them at http://www.christianitytoday.com/international.

The Lausanne Movement

As Billy Graham preached around the world from the 1940s through the 1960s, he developed a passion to "unite all evangelicals in the common task of the total evangelization of the world." In 1966 the Billy Graham Evangelistic Association, in partnership with *Christianity Today* magazine, sponsored the World Congress on Evangelism in Berlin. That congress brought together twelve hundred delegates from more than one hundred countries and inspired an explosion in global evangelistic outreach.

Just a few years later, Graham perceived the need for a larger, more diverse congress to reframe the Christian mission of evangelization in a world rife with social, political, economic, and religious upheaval. He shared this idea with one hundred world Christian leaders, and the affirmation of the need for such a congress was overwhelmingly enthusiastic.

In July 1974, twenty-seven hundred participants from more than 150 nations gathered in Lausanne, Switzerland, for ten days of discussion, fellowship, worship, and prayer. The congress achieved an unprecedented diversity of nationalities, ethnicities, ages, occupations, and denominational affiliations. A reporter from *Time* magazine described the Lausanne Congress as "a formidable forum, possibly the widest-ranging meeting of Christians ever held."[1]

The outcome was a unification behind the vision to reach the world for Christ, and also the production of the groundbreaking Lausanne Covenant, which declared the statement of faith and goals of the Christian evangelical community.

Today, the Lausanne Movement continues to inspire collaboration and cooperation among Bible-believing Christians around the globe. The Lausanne Web site gives leaders access to current and historical information on global evangelization; information about national, regional, and international gatherings; and theological and practical research and information.

The Connect section on the Web site offers ways to interact regionally with Lausanne Movement leaders. In addition, visitors can learn more about a wide range of global issues related to world evangelization in which Lausanne is engaged, and find ways to connect with others involved in those issues.

To receive current information about the Lausanne Movement, and evangelization efforts, subscribe online at www.lausanne.org. There you can subscribe to the Lausanne *Connecting Point* e-newsletter, a free monthly publication. Lausanne also provides the free monthly online magazine *Lausanne World Pulse* (LWP), offering missions and evangelism news, information, and analysis from leaders around the world.

LWP is a collaborative partnership between Lausanne and the Institute of Strategic Evangelism and the Evangelism and Missions Information Service (Wheaton College, Wheaton, Illinois). *Lausanne World Pulse* is offered online, through an RSS feed or e-mail alert, and as a downloadable executive summary print version for reading offline.

For more information, visit http://www.lausanne.org.

Recommended Networking and Web Evangelism Help Sites

Web Evangelism Tools

Internet Evangelism Day: http://www.internetevangelismday.com/
    index.php
Internet Evangelism Network: http://www.webevangelism.com
CBN.com Evangelism Resources: http://cbn.com/spirituallife/Church
    AndMinistry/evangelism/index.aspx

CBN.com Share Your Faith: http://cbn.com/spirituallife/shareyourfaith

GUIDE Network: http://www.internetevangelismday.com/guide-network.php

Web Evangelism Guide by Tony Whittaker: http://www.web-evangelism.com

Internet Ministry Conference: http://www.internetevangelismday.com/events.php

Cybermissions.org: http://www.cybermissions.org

American Tract Society: http://www.atstracts.org/internet

Apologetics Toolbox: http://www.apologeticstoolbox.com

Online Training for Online Evangelists: http://www.webevangelism.com/otoe/index.php

E-vangelism by Andrew Careage: http://www.e-vangelism.com

Evangelism Toolbox: http://www.evangelismtoolbox.com

Preparing Your Personal Testimony: http://www.5clicks.com

Ron Hutchcraft Ministries: http://www.hutchcraft.com

Leonard Sweet: http://www.leonardsweet.com

Pew Internet and American Life Project: http://www.pewinternet.org/index.asp

Quentin Schultze: http://www.quentinschultze.com

Top Chretien: http://www.topchretien.com

TruthMedia Internet Group: http://truthmedia.com/index.php

Way of the Master with Ray Comfort and Kirk Cameron: http://www.wayofthemaster.com

Probe Ministries: http://www.probe.org

Dare2Share: http://www.dare2share.org

Evangelism Explosion: http://www.eeinternational.org

Gospel.com Apologetics Index: http://www.gospel.com/topics/apologetics

Bryan Turner Evangelism 101: http://www.bryanturner.org/evangelism101/index.htm

InterVarsity's QuestioningFaith.com: http://www.ivpress.com/questioningfaith/resources

Apologetics Index: http://www.apologeticsindex.org

Software, Webmaster, and Technical Advice

Christian Web Masters: www.christian-web-masters.net/forums

Webmaster Talk: www.webmaster-talk.com

Great Church Websites: www.greatchurchwebsites.org

ChurchMedia.net: www.ChurchMedia.net

SiteProNews' Webmaster articles: www.sitepronews.com/article-archives

SitePro newsletters: www.sitepronews.com/archives.html

SitePoint: www.sitepoint.com/newsletter

StockExchange graphics: www.sxc.hu

Firefox browser Add-ons: https://addons.mozilla.org/en-US/firefox

International Conference on Computing and Mission (ICCM):
www.iccm.org

Chapter Eleven

As the Waters Cover the Seas: NetCasting to the World

Carmella had not heard from her cousin Estelle in Cuba since she fled the country thirty-six years ago. Then one day, without notice, Carmella received Estelle's e-mail address from a mutual friend in Costa Rica and the two began corresponding. With the connection reestablished, they looked forward to their weekly e-mails.

They began the process of catching up on the events of nearly four decades in their lives. Soon Carmella arrived at the time when she received Jesus as her Savior. From that point on, most of their e-mails centered on what God was doing to bring peace and joy in her life and in the life of her family.

Estelle said that she waited for Carmella's e-mail as if it was an episode from a novel. One day Carmella sent the sinner's prayer and the meaning of being born again. In the next e-mail Carmella received, Estelle said that she and her husband had prayed the prayer and were planning to go to a house church on Sunday. She was also talking to her children and their spouses, sharing the gospel with them so they, too, would come to know Christ.

Estelle had been raised Roman Catholic, and her husband had been an atheist. After she prayed to receive Jesus as her Savior, Estelle dug out her mother's Bible and began reading it with her husband.

That was the last e-mail Carmella received from Estelle. After that the communication was cut off. She hasn't heard from her dear cousin since, but she prays for her and for her family, that the seeds sown through this Internet connection will take root and that the entire family will come to know freedom in Christ.

The Mission of Internet Evangelism

I remember pondering in the early 1990s what a blessing e-mail would be for missionaries on the field. The fact that they could more easily send and receive correspondence and assistance via the Internet thrilled me.

Today the number of tools available for missionaries and global NetCasters is truly staggering. The explosion of the information age has given missionaries opportunities for outreach that they would have never dreamed of only two decades ago.

And these ministry opportunities are not limited to the cities anymore. Any remote location that can connect to the digital grid via satellite or a digital cell phone signal can go online and be in touch with half of the population of planet Earth!

But of course there is much more opportunity to connect with people who are in the world's cities—and more people are now living in cities than ever before. I believe the intersecting of the mass exodus to the cities by the world's population and the advent of the Internet and mobile digital media is part of God's strategy to make Himself known to mankind in these last days.

We are living in a day of destiny!

The world has never been more connected than it is right now. The global village is rapidly shrinking. The political, economic, religious, and cultural barriers that have hindered the spread of the gospel are coming down.

John Edmiston of Cybermissions.org believes that the Internet offers enormous potential for ministry across cultural barriers, and that in many countries the Internet is a more secure way to share the gospel than is the presence of a Western missionary. "Truths of the gospel are universal. We need to be prepared for people who ask different questions based on their culture. The power of the Word of God on the Internet has a 24/7 impact." But he cautions Christians who share their faith online to effectively address cultural differences and not just present a 'westernized' gospel translated into another language. "The gospel," he emphasizes, "needs to be incarnated into each culture."[1]

Reversing the Tower of Babel

This amazing testimony from Groundwire.net demonstrates the power and beauty of the Internet.

Jeremy M: Hello, Jose. So what's your question about salvation?

Jose: How are u saved?

Jeremy M: Well, salvation comes by accepting the sacrifice of Jesus paying the price for your sins on the cross. It's not complicated; it's just a matter of accepting the free gift of the salvation He provided.

The Bible says that if we believe in our hearts that Jesus died for our sins and God raised Him from the dead, and if we confess that with our mouths, then we receive salvation. It's a matter of asking Jesus to come into your heart with your mouth, and making sure that your heart is in agreement with those words.

Would you like to accept Jesus as your Lord and secure your eternal salvation?

Jose: Yes, do u have a Spanish speaker?

Jeremy M: Hmmm, not someone fluent. Is your English OK or do you need it in Spanish?

Jose: In Spanish, my English is really broke.

Jeremy M: OK, can you give me a minute to take care of that for you?

Jose: Sorry.

Jeremy M: It's OK. You will have to forgive me, but the best I can do will probably be a broken Spanish translation. Let me post it, and you can let me know if what I am saying makes sense, OK?

Jose: OK.

Using the translator at Babblefish.com, Jeremy (a non-Spanish speaker) shared the plan of salvation with Jose—and then led him to Christ in Spanish!

Jeremy M: . . . *Creo que resucitaron de los muertos, está vivo, y oye a su hijo, Jesús Cristo muerto por mis pecados, mi rezo* . . . Does that make sense to you?

Jose: Yes. Do I pray?

Jeremy M: Then pray that prayer out loud, and get your heart to agree with those words I posted. Pray that prayer above that I posted in Spanish. Can you do that?

Jose: Yes, it's better for me.

Jeremy M: Then let me know after you have prayed that prayer out loud to God, OK?

Jose: Amen.

Jeremy M: Good, Jose. You made a very good choice today. Do you know anyone who is saved?

Jose: *Pastor es buen ayuda. Si, yo tengo salvado?*

Jeremy M: Are you asking if you are saved?

Jose: I saved now, no?

Jeremy M: *Si!*

Jose: *Gracias, Buenos noches.*

Jeremy M: *Tenga una buena tarde, amigo.*

Missions and Internet Evangelism

Because the Internet is worldwide in its reach, Internet evangelists need to understand and plan for the fact that they can potentially connect with people all around the globe. John Edmiston uses his Web site, cybermisions.org, to train Internet evangelists to take the gospel to the nations. He also works with missionaries to establish Internet cafés on the user end, many of which are in countries difficult to reach by normal missionary means.

"We set up an Internet café and give a group of local missionaries, not Western ones, some twenty computers and technical help. Through the twenty computers they get a little bit of income and that enables them to run it as a business. So, of course, in some of these unreached areas we don't give them a name like 'Converting the World to Jesus Internet Café,' because that would ensure the place would be burned down. It just looks like a normal business."

Edmiston has set up twelve Internet cafés worldwide and is working on another sixteen, with quite a few more planned in different parts of the globe. In these tough-to-evangelize areas, the people running each café engage in what he calls "friendship evangelism."

"You have to go very slowly in most areas and you certainly don't bash them over the head with a Bible when they're sitting there at a computer. People go in there to check their e-mail and they're in there two or three times a week, and so friendships are built that way. As our person realizes that one is a genuine seeker, not a plant or a government agent, they would go into a one-on-one discipleship process and once they're trusted, they go into a house church. You have to be very security conscious through the whole process."

When I asked Tony Whittaker what parts of the world are ripe for Internet evangelism, he responded, "Which ones aren't?"

"I've tried to highlight Japan as particularly needy, owing to being so highly wired, so minimally Christian, and unable to easily access English language material. The Mideast—as you know, many incredible things are happening. By and large, the West is now wired. There will not be much more Web growth here. North America, Western Europe, Australia, and New Zealand, plus Japan and Korea are highly wired. The Middle East is quite so. Eastern Europe is growing. South America is quite wired and still growing.

"The next billion users will come from the non-western world, and will be a completely different demographic; poor, or relatively so, less literate, not first-language English speakers. They will access the Web through Internet cafes and increasingly through mobile phones. Their needs, and therefore effective, appropriate Web evangelism, will be very different.

"Missionaries have been intrigued by the prospect of Internet evangelism. But incorporating IE into their overall mission strategy has proven to be a big challenge.

"I wish it would happen more," Whittaker laments. "One way would be to create local interest blogs or community sites. Powertochange.com has offered their material to be branded into a locality-based Web site."

Internet and Media Outreach to Muslims

God is pouring out His Spirit in amazing ways around the world—and in particular to Muslims. Reports are flooding in from the Islamic world of people coming to Christ after dreams and visions of Jesus appearing to them. And recently there has also been an explosion of evangelistic activity in the Muslim world through the Internet, satellite television, SMS text, and mobile telephones.

The religious walls that have kept Muslims bound in ancient lies are being penetrated and torn down by the Holy Spirit, in part through media ministry. The imams and the dictators can't stay ahead of the rapidly changing technology. So today, thanks to the Internet and satellite TV, the gospel message is being preached with power in the Muslim nations that once would not allow it.

I spoke with a NetCaster and broadcaster—I'll call him Talal—about the synergy of ministry that's converging to lead Muslims around the globe to Christ.

von Buseck: You have discovered a very effective way to bring synergy between the television and the Internet.

Talal: About four years ago I heard about this show that was being done by a Coptic priest that was very effective in the Muslim world. His unique approach was to read the Islamic books and highlight and expose some of the teachings that Islam believes in, and Islam is teaching, and Islam is practicing. So the name of the show was Questions About

Faith. So they would take topics that are taboo or are not allowed to be discussed or even questioned in Islam and discuss them.

Eventually this caused an uproar in the Middle East. Then the show started to receive a lot of response. So I contacted this ministry and I said, "How can I help you?" We started partnering and producing these shows. We improved the quality.

We started to come out with new ideas. The approach is very effective. Basically instead of playing defense as Christians—always defending the Bible—we started playing defense and offense. So we started saying, "OK, here is the answer to what you asked us. Now let us ask you about this." So the television ministry is starting to boom.

Then we came out with a new program called *In the Bull's Eye*, which takes pure Islamic topics, like, for example, the birth of Muhammad. According to Islamic teachings, he was born four years after his dad died. For the Muslims to clarify the subject, they said it's OK for a woman to have a baby as long as it's before four years—she can be pregnant for four years. In fact, there are fatwas from the highest Islamic schools that say, yes, a woman can be pregnant for four years—which is against every scientific and human possibility.

Then we came out with a program called *Truth Talk*, where we would interview a Muslim background believer and talk about their experience to show the Muslim world that Muslims are coming to Christ.

Then we started producing another show called *Taking Off the Mask*, which takes current events, analyzes them, and then talks about the root cause of these events—and why Muslims believe this and why it is happening this way.

So after doing all these shows—and they were so effective—then we moved into the live shows where Muslims can call and ask about anything, from Islamic or Christian topics. And praise God, so many people are coming to Christ. So many Muslims are coming out of Islam, and they are saying, "I can't believe I used to believe this. I can't believe that my mom and dad still believe in this."

We are launching our third live show. The program *Truth Talk*, that we started as a taped show, is going to turn into a live show.

People respond in different ways. People respond via e-mail, phone, letters, and the Web site. We receive e-mails from all over the world. On a daily basis we receive one thousand e-mails, and this is a conservative number. These are ministry e-mails and also comments from the Web site.

During the live show, we will receive between three hundred and nine hundred e-mails in an hour and a half. And these people are calling country to country. So people in the Muslim world are calling a U.K. number or a French number. These are not local numbers, so it costs people a lot of money. But this is like a lifeline for people. And the telephone ministry—and I call it telephone ministry because it started as support for the live shows—is now turning into its own ministry.

von Buseck: How are you using the Internet in your strategy?

Talal: You really cannot separate the Internet from the satellite. The Internet is our number one means of feedback and way to get instant reports and communication from our audience. Now unfortunately, throughout the Muslim world, so many countries are blocking the Internet. But technology, in most cases, is ahead of people blocking Web sites. There is always somehow, somewhere that people can find ways around it to send messages and e-mail.

We made a documentary on Jihad. It's a one-and-a-half-hour documentary that is, in my opinion, the best analysis, description, and explanation about Jihad, with English subtitles. It's in Arabic. We aired it on Thanksgiving. In a matter of eight days, out of our Web site, more than one million people downloaded the program. That tells you that people are looking for good-quality productions. People are looking for information. People are looking for answers. And when people download it, they put it on their own Web sites and then they distribute it.

It's amazing what God is doing through this whole thing. What the Lord is putting on our heart is not a matter of language; it's a matter of knowledge. Without knowledge people would perish. It's to make this information that is working so powerfully in the Arabic-speaking world, for God to give us wisdom in the English-speaking world and beyond.

We are creating an Internet community and a message system for people to leave comments and to evaluate things. Every once in a while we post surveys. We post music videos and teachings. So we are using a lot of different mechanisms. We transcribe all of our episodes so that people can view them online. This is all posted on www.Islamexplained. com. We have both Arabic and English versions of this Web site.

von Buseck: Including the work you are doing, what do you see as the most effective Internet strategies for reaching Muslims with the gospel at this point?

Talal: Communities. Create a community. Don't make it a one-way preaching podium.

von Buseck: So Web 2.0 for Muslims.

Talal: Absolutely. People like to make it a two-way community and strategy. Keep the levels of respect. Allow people to share their views and opinions. Honestly, as Christians, there shouldn't be anything that we should be unwilling to face, ask, or question. And be transparent. Be yourself. If you don't know, say you don't know. Ask someone. Be yourself—don't have this teacher mentality.

von Buseck: How are you utilizing SMS text and mobile?

Talal: We really are researching this because we are in a unique situation. We can't just use SMS anywhere. We have to keep some levels of security. Our coverage goes over the whole Middle East, Iran, North Africa, Europe, North America, and Australia. It's almost impossible to be able to do it all like this. So we need a system that will work in all of these places. So we are working on it and we are studying different options.

von Buseck: Can you think of any e-mail or chat experiences that stand out as individual testimonies?

Talal: A lady sent us a very long e-mail from a Muslim country, telling us her story. She was the daughter of an imam of a mosque. She and two of her siblings specialized and had college degrees in Islamic studies. Her main mission in life was to reach out to Christians. Each of the three took a different people group. One of them was for the Shiites—they consider the Shiites as non-Muslim. Another one was for the secular. And she was for the Christians.

This lady started listening to our television shows and getting angry and cursing the host and the other guests. She couldn't even stand to watch them on television. She would go and pray and curse them more. Then she started to listen more.

Then she started to doubt. Then she started to read more. Then she went to the Web site and watched every single episode. Then she wanted to know and research her religion and she found out that we're right. She started to ask more and more.

Then Jesus showed her in a dream and a vision, Himself in a desert, that He is God, and He is the true one she is looking for.

She started writing and corresponding with Christians in Lebanon. Then she went to Lebanon and met these people. She sent to us this wonderful e-mail to thank us for all the shows and to tell us her life story. In this whole life story she mentioned that she's a wonderful believer in Christ. She's still hidden in her job and her Islamic traditions at home. Our shows on television are the only church she has now, and her only comfort. It's a powerful e-mail and a powerful story.

So people are watching us, corresponding by e-mail. This e-mail and the television are their spiritual lifeline.

von Buseck: Who else is doing effective Internet evangelism to Muslims, but maybe a little differently than we are doing?

Talal: There are quite a few people—on an individual level, on a ministry level, on a church level—doing Internet outreach to Muslims. God is bringing unity, networking, and unification into all these groups to work together.

von Buseck: What are some of their techniques that maybe wouldn't work for us, but they are working for them?

Talal: It's not techniques, it's more like specialties. Some people are focusing on correspondence in different areas of the world. Others are producing just Christian shows. Other people are focusing on producing children's shows. Other people are focusing on women. There is overlap—like our ministry and another ministry focusing on exposing Islam—going down to the roots and talking Islamic topics. Not everyone has the resources or the ability to do it, and God has blessed us with outlets to air these shows. Maybe the how-to comes second, but first comes the message and who is your target audience.

von Buseck: If there are people out there who have a passion to reach Muslims for Christ and they're not a part of another group, what are some ways that they can, on their own, start reaching out through the Web to other Muslims?

Talal: That is what I'm really trying to avoid, and I don't honestly encourage, which is to try to do it yourself. There is a lot attached to it—security, information, accountability. There is no lone-star Texas Ranger anymore. And even larger media organizations cannot do it alone. So it doesn't matter if it's an individual or a church or an organization—no one can do it on their own.

Digital Jungles: Taking the Internet to Rural Lands

While missionaries have been involved in Internet evangelism for years in urban settings like these Internet cafés, exciting opportunities are also beginning to open up for remote Internet evangelism. This will most likely happen through Internet cafés that are linked to satellite or cell connections and are powered by solar panels—or it will be through mobile digital devices.

"Almost the entire population of the world now lives in a mobile phone reception area," says Tony Whittaker. "India has decided to wire up the entire nation with broadband Web, free. Presumably this is going to include a considerable use of WiFi. This is a megaopportunity."

Dave Hackett of VisionSynergy commented that he thought that the mobile device, with foldable keyboard, may well replace the laptop concept, as both a usable computing device as well as being a phone, video/mp3 player, and much else.

One example of the innovative ways missionaries are beginning to connect remote areas to the rest of the world is a project called Link Net that is being developed deep in the jungles of Zambia by NetCaster Jonathan Backens.

Link Net was pioneered by a Dutch entrepreneur named Gertjan, a Christian who is trained professionally in telecommunications. Gertjan's wife, Janika, is a medical doctor who wanted to do work in Africa. God gave Gertjan the idea to use telecommunications as a way to transform

Africa. The Lord opened an opportunity for Janika to do rural malaria research in a remote village in Zambia, six hours outside Lusaka, the capital. It is two hours by car from a paved road or a telephone.

"You get there by a 4 x 4 or by a Cessna 206," Backens explains. "You land in a handmade airstrip. It took a hundred men a year to build it. You fly in to the capital and then Flying Mission, a missions support agency that flies missionaries all over the place, picks you up from there."

Gertjan had the idea of bringing in Internet computers to develop a community center. The people who don't work at the hospital are at the poverty level or below. Gertjan talked to the head man who gave him an old building used to store grain. Gertjan called friends from the Netherlands to raise money, and he completely renovated it. He built the Internet café and began training locals.

The research hospital likes it because they do rural communications. It connects these Western doctors with their home base. "So essentially, the hospital pays for the initial satellite feed," Backens explains. "They pay for the Internet connection and they let our Internet café feed off it. The café is essentially self-sustaining now. We're projecting that it will take about two years for these Internet cafes to become economically viable.

"So Gertjan came in and did this about two years ago. He brought in the first satellite feed. And there are about twenty-five computers. He added to that a radio station and a small library. There is a shop for the women of the area who sell handwoven baskets.

"The big cities have been reached. The rural villages have not, because it takes time and it takes years of going there. So that's where we want to go. We want to go rural. Over the next four to five years we want to have twenty-five self-sufficient, working sites."

Building Indispensable Partnerships

Evangelism is all about relationship: with God, with those you are witnessing to, and with other Christians of similar vision. Dave Hackett has a vision for empowering missionaries to use the Internet as a tool of outreach. The key, he explains, is bringing groups together in what he calls "indispensable partnerships."

"First, you need to know the key players," Hackett explains. "The due diligence phase is a lot of research. Most people look only for the biggest players, and somehow learn what they are doing, and maybe try to interact with them. Our approach is to find as many as we can— look over the whole spectrum and find out what is going on. We've got a directory of non-English Internet evangelism Web sites—1,300 in 860 languages, all listed and sorted."

Hackett encourages ministries to know the field better than anybody so they can build effective partnerships and can avoid duplicating efforts. Hackett gave an example of why this is important for effective outreach. "At an Internet evangelism conference, a ministry presented its downloadable-to-cell-phone Arabic Bible. These Web evangelists were very proud of it. It had been successfully downloaded ten thousand times over eight months, primarily on the Arabian Peninsula. It's a great tool."

But when Hackett asked them how they compared and contrasted their tool with the six or eight other Arabic downloadable-to-cell-phone Bibles, their jaws dropped. "They had done virtually no research. It didn't even cross their minds to do a Google search on the topic. If they had done even that rudimentary due diligence, they could have said, 'Ah, this is the thing that we really can build on and further the whole offering.'

"So one key way that we approach the Internet is to change the default question from, 'I have a vision for a ministry; how can I work on it?' to, 'I've got an exciting vision for ministry; who else might be working on this? Who else might share this vision?'

"I started cataloging all the various ways Christians are using mobile platform pieces for evangelism. I created a mobile evangelism wiki (http://snipr.com/mobileev). For the first time, to my knowledge, I've aggregated links and descriptions of the variety of ways that ministries were trying to adapt mobile. It's open for editing, and we've got people around the world who are putting up additional things."

Hackett quickly built up a list of practitioners and started contacting them. "These people felt like they were a lone guy doing this. So it has been very exciting to talk to these people. Most of them are Chief Executive Officers (CEOs), Chief Internet Officers (CIOs), or Chief Technology Officers (CTOs)—they are entrepreneurs or ministries. They have their own means and hopes, and we have been sensing that they can connect. They can do better."

Jesus commanded the church to take the gospel to every people group, tribe, and tongue. Through the Internet, mobile digital devices, and satellite television, we now have the tools in our hands to take one giant step toward the fulfillment of this command.

Will you be one of the NetCasters who will see this happen in your lifetime? I pray that you will be—and that through the efforts of both the air forces and the ground troops, "For the earth will be filled with the knowledge of the Lord's glory, as the waters cover the sea" (Hab. 2:14).

Chapter Twelve

Go Ye and Make NetCasters

When Jesus said in the Great Commission, "Go, therefore, and make disciples," He was indirectly saying, "Go, therefore, and make NetCasters," because every believer is called by God to publicly declare the gospel of Jesus Christ. We are all called to cast our nets—the question is where He wants us to cast them.

Now through the Internet and digital technology, every person is enabled to literally go into all the world! Millions of Christians log on to the Internet on an ongoing basis. For most people forty and younger, at least in the West, being on the Web is a way of life—and it is increasingly common for the forty-and-over crowd as well. It is now time to go beyond looking to the Internet to meet our needs—it's time to begin caring for the needs of the millions of lost and hurting people who surf the Web every day.

Let the NetCaster Revolution Begin

With millions seeking spiritual truth on the Internet, there is now an incredible opportunity for evangelism and discipleship through digital devices. Every ten minutes, 460 new people use the Web for the first time.[1] Now is the time for individual Christians, local churches, parachurch ministries, and media ministries to reach out to these folks as true NetCasters—harnessing the power of the Internet to take the gospel to the ends of the earth.

Web evangelism gives believers opportunities to reach these people with the gospel right where they are, just as Jesus and Paul did. The worldwide impact of the Internet and the digital revolution will be as far-reaching—and most likely more so—as the invention of the printing press and the satellite dish. How the church uses this vibrant communication tool today could shape the fate of mankind for thousands of years to come.

"For the vast majority of Christians, the sunset version of what is happening ('The world has come to an end') eclipses the dawn version ('It's a whole new world out there')" Christian futurist Leonard Sweet observes. "In a church blind to the world it is in, where it mistakes the dawn for a setting sun, those with open eyelids must reconcile themselves to the role of either seeing-eye dogs or bloodhound . . . How leaders of the church can sleepwalk into this future is beyond comprehension."[2]

With a hint of sadness, Sweet observes, "How many church leaders are on the short list of people who are changing the world?"[3]

But it doesn't have to be this way in the body of Christ. The time has come for Christians to make a difference in this world by embracing these monumental changes and harnessing them to see the fulfillment of the Great Commission. There is a need for the church to begin using the Internet and digital media as a means for taking the gospel to the nations.

I believe there is much hope in store for the world and the church—if only believers would leave the "stained glass" behind and take the gospel out into the world of the "plain glass."

Sadly, the greatest hindrances to the church catching this vision is a combined fear of the dangers associated with the Internet (they are real, but we must confront them rather than run from them), and an eschato-logical belief in the world continuing to decline without hope until Jesus returns, causing in some a feeling of hopelessness and surrender to the evil in the world.

Western Christianity must also battle a fixation with materialism and self-centered success, causing an inward view toward self instead of an outward view toward the lost. This "me" mentality often results in a lack of vision for the church to utilize technology, travel, and communication breakthrough to see the Great Commission fulfilled.

As Leonard Sweet points out, the world gets it—the church doesn't . . . yet.

But visionaries and pioneers in the world and in the church understand that we are in a momentous shift in technology, philosophy, and spirituality—one that rivals all other great shifts in human history.

One of the early employees of Apple Inc. said of founder Steve Jobs and his colleagues, "[Our] fundamental purpose was to innovate, invent, and lead an entire cultural revolution . . . All the people I met there, passionate young people, truly believed they were changing the world, not selling computers."[4]

The church in the new millennium must adopt this same mind-set toward the lost. What we do—in whatever area that each is called to by the Holy Spirit—can and will change the world with God's grace and anointing.

Bold Christian leaders who have not hidden behind the stained glass—those who have taken Christ's admonition to be in the world, but not of it; to be salt and light, not hiding the light under a basket—are stepping out into the calling that God has for their lives. They are asking God to give them creativity, strategies, wisdom, provision, and anointing to do the task ahead of them.

This may be a relatively small number of people compared to the millions of Christians around the world, but it's remarkable what can be done when a group of believers step out in faith, trusting the Word of the Lord—just look at the early disciples.

The NetCaster Uprising

Internet evangelism pioneers are paving the way, crying out to the church, "Things don't have to be like this. People who have lived in darkness can now see the Light—through the light of their computer screen!"

Now we need rank-and-file Christians to capture the vision of using every tool on the Internet and mobile media to take the gospel to the ends of the earth.

Using the latest technology to spread the gospel has been part of God's evangelism strategy for the church since the beginning. Throughout church history, Christians have harnessed the power of technology to make the gospel relevant and accessible to their generation. In the last one hundred years, modern innovations in radio, film, television, air transportation, and satellite communication made it possible to quickly and efficiently take the gospel around the world—reaching more people than earlier generations would have dreamed possible.

It appears that God has once again taken us beyond our wildest dreams by giving us the Internet as a dynamic evangelistic tool—a means of communication that synchronizes all previous media tools and makes them available to all people in their own languages.

Today more people are accepting Christ through relationships built on the Internet than ever before—and the church is just scratching the surface of what is possible!

Final Fishing Tips from the NetCasters

In order to catch fish, a NetCaster must know where the fish are gathering and what kind of bait they're hitting on. Tony Whittaker encourages NetCasters to draw the lines of contextualization in evangelism wide in order to relate to seekers online and lead them to Christ. "The problem with the Western church is that we have not really learned the lessons that the missions community has done over the last century and more, in terms of,

- learning and studying the culture;
- presenting the gospel in contextualized terms; and
- understanding people groups, and how the gospel usually flows across relationships with people who are within the same or a similar cultural group.

"Mike Frost, an Australian missiologist, has pointed out that the era of 'Christendom is over—get used to it.' We need to use the missiology insights and techniques that have been employed in the last fifty years in missions outreach to reach the Western church. The tendency is just to do the same stuff that used to work. Or we think used to work. Just shout a bit louder."

"There is going to have to be some change at the top of a lot of organizations for it to really take off," says Debra Brown of Hope House Church in Second Life. "But then there is this viral thing. The *Time* person of the year was who? It was you. And that is kind of the essence of the change we see. It is the power of one. And really one person can reach the whole world.

"You put the right video on YouTube and all of a sudden you are a hero for the day and everybody in the world is watching your video. The tipping point is you—and you and you and you. People like us.

"Who am I? I'm just some person who's doing an MDiv. But it's people like me—or the Tony Whittakers who just sit behind a computer—and now we have Internet Evangelism Day."

"I'm forty-eight," says Drew Dickens of NeedHim.com, "and enough of my brain is still driving a Monte Carlo in high school that I can still fake my way, with a straight face. I can talk to postmoderns and seem almost relevant. But I'm having to push. I'm having to stretch to do that.

"There is a site called notreligion.com that we use as a model of postmodernism. It's something that we constantly have to remember. If I'm going to design sites, they're going to look like a forty-eight-year-old, and we're going to have *Just as I Am* playing in the background—without meaning to. So it's a constant push for us to stay relevant to that group.

"Postmoderns are not going to read through ten pages of text to get the gospel. I'm constantly searching YouTube for just homemade junk that speaks to this culture. It's relevant. It's compelling. It's edgy. It's fresh. So we're looking to do something with YouTube as well."

When talking about how to motivate people to get involved in Internet evangelism, Dickens quotes Ron Hutchcraft. "If you don't have the want-to, the how-to doesn't matter.

"It's so true. We spend so much time talking about what color our site is. Should I use *Sharing Jesus without Fear?* Should I use Alpha? Should I use this verse or that verse? We spend way too much time on the how-to. My question to him has always been, 'How do you frame the want-to?'"

"I can frame the how-to. I'm ordained and I have the diplomas on my walls, from Evangelism Explosion and everybody else. I always tell this to our volunteers who come to us all nervous about how-to. I tell them, 'Here's what's going to happen. We're gonna give you a script. You'll read it once and you'll throw it away. That's fine. That's what we want you to do. You'll get on a call and you're going to quote Romans 6:23 rather than 3:23, and you'll say Ephesians 2:9–10 instead of 4–8. And all of a sudden the caller is going to start crying and say, 'Yes, that's what I want.' And you realize, 'It's not anything I said.' It's not the how-to, it's the want-to."

How does a NetCaster get a Christian to the moment of clarity when he decides, "I've got to do this"?

Dickens answered, "The prophet Nathan came to David and set him up. I did that in a Sunday school class. I set them up. I asked what would they do if they had a friend who said, 'I'm just not sensing God at work in my life.' What are some things they would tell the friend to do? So the class said this and that, and then somebody said, 'I'd tell them to share their faith.' So I pulled the whole Nathan thing and said, 'You're the friend.'

"I've told people from the sales perspective we all ask ourselves, 'What's in it for me?' So what's in it for me to share my faith online? You need to be prepared to answer that question. You know what it's like when you share your faith. Talk about some of those benefits. Some people may be convicted by the fact that it's a command. For some it's a form of worship. Being 'guilted' into it, that's worked for us before.

"Somehow you need to find a way to force them to look at themselves and realize what they're not doing. Campus Crusade did a survey and found that only 1 to 10 percent of Christians are active in sharing their faith. That information may compel people to say 'Wow, I need to do more of that kind of thing.'"

Dickens quoted Spurgeon who said, "If the lost be damned, let them leap into hell over our bodies as we are grasping at their ankles. For let no one go there un-prayed-for or uninformed."[5]

"That carries with it a certain level of the attitude that 'You're going to hell through me. If you go, you're going through me first.' That takes a certain level of passion that a lot of people don't have.

"Testimonies are powerful," Dickens concluded. "We're much more motivated to help the one than the thousands. We see the picture or hear the story of the hungry child. Here's the child in my lap. We can hear that millions die or millions go hungry, but it changes when you see the one child on someone's lap. So I think testimonies that talk about the one are powerful."

Return on Evangelism Investment

Talking about the 1.3 million people who received Christ through Campus Crusade's online Global Media Outreach in 2007, Allan Beeber observed, "There are people on the boards of these ministries who are business people and will look at this when they eventually get the data. Unfortunately most ministries either don't have that type of data or are not reporting it. But once thinking chairmen and members of the board begin asking the right questions, they're going to be saying, 'Wait a minute, you're telling me that for thirty thousand dollars, which is equivalent of half a staff member, we saw as much evangelism as an entire ministry? And we can track this? Why aren't we doing more of this?'

"Of course, you're always going to have the perception, especially by the older generation, that these are electronic. They aren't real people. But you read the e-mails and you say, 'Uh, I'm sorry, these are real.'

"So the technology is the only thing that's changed. Long-distance evangelism and discipleship are the biblical model. And we cannot have a computer answer people. We need to have real people answering people, using the computer. The expression is—and it is not something I came up with, I'm simply repeating it—our strategy involves using high touch with high tech. And I'd say that's essential."

Just Do It

Johnnie Gnanamanickam points out that one of the most important things to remember when diving into evangelism through the Internet and Web 2.0 is to experiment. "Don't try to get it all right. Start small. Do something today and just keep innovating. Incremental change is what you need, so keep trying several things.

"Start out small, but be ready to scale quickly, because some of those ideas flop and don't go anywhere, and some of those become YouTube and are really big. And when they get really big, it happens overnight. So that's generally the thing to do. Just pray for direction and do something today. Ask the Lord for direction and don't worry about being perfect. Do something today and keep building on that.

"Keep doing the things that work. And throw away the things that don't."

John Sorensen of Evangelism Explosion is excited at the potential the Internet holds for taking the Word to the world. "I think that the Internet has made possible the land of the storyteller again. I think we're getting back to the day and age when a storyteller will once again be king, if you will.

"You look at the stuff that's popular on YouTube today, and it is the folks who really have the ability to capture somebody with a story. There are very few how-to type things that people are going to go to. I don't think you're going to see a how-to video become popular—unless it's how to do something that's radical or weird.

"But you can capture the world with a story.

"For a long time there wasn't the avenue that a person had to release something worldwide as it is right now. We've seen a lot of industries shift. There used to be a day when in order to be an audio or a video engineer you had to be a technician. You had to have a pocket protector and tweak your knobs, and stuff like that. It didn't used to be that way. It used to be that you had a flatbed, and it was the storyteller who got to do the editing. In today's world, the technology has been given back again. The storyteller has the tools. You can create movies in today's world.

"You can create a movie today with a high-definition camcorder. That's the world we live in. And the sooner that people realize that they have that kind of capacity to engage that kind of an audience with a story, we'll begin to raise up and applaud storytellers.

"I think it's an exciting time for us," Sorensen explains, "because, frankly, we've got the greatest story ever told. We've got the corner on the truth. So bring it on. Within Christian ministry we've got to applaud that. We've got to expose that. We've got to lift up young men and women who are going to be able to tell phenomenal stories."

Dr. Sterling Huston of the Digital Evangelism Network anticipates great things ahead for those who will take seriously God's call to evangelize the world through the World Wide Web.

"We have seen dramatic change in the last ten years from when Web first became available publicly and we saw that 100 million people were suddenly online. That has only accelerated over those ten years to the 1.7 billion approximately online now. It is moving from what was dominated by English as the primary language, to now Chinese is the second largest language on the Web. I believe the center of gravity of activity for this is actually moving to Asia where they have such great technological growth.

"Just as we've seen dramatic growth in the last ten years, I believe the growth will be even more dramatic in the next ten years. My great concern is that the church will get so far behind the curve that it cannot catch up. My great vision is that we can stimulate and release a lot of entrepreneurial individuals, organizations, and churches to say, 'This gives us a tool and an outreach to fulfill what is Jesus' timeless mission to take the gospel to the ends of the earth. And not only to take the gospel there, but also to provide a mechanism that begins the process of making disciples in every tongue and every nation.'"

The Implications of the NetCaster Revolution

I am convinced that we are at a dramatic crossroads at the dawn of this new millennium. In philosophy, Western thought has shifted from modern to postmodern. In technology, we have shifted from analogue to digital. We have shifted from the Industrial to the digital age. In the church, I believe we are shifting from a pastoral-centered focus to a truly fivefold-centered practice—from the ministry of the professional clergy and parachurch worker to the ministry of the saints.

And now is the time for the saints to grab the reins of digital technology and run with the Good News of salvation through Jesus Christ!

This is a climactic, five-hundred-year shift, more dramatic even than the shift from medieval times to the era of the Enlightenment.

Unlike many Christians today, I don't believe that the world will continue to grow darker unchecked until the earth is filled with evil and followers of Jesus Christ are hunkered down in caves, waiting and praying for the Rapture. Scripture tells us, "The path of the righteous is like the light of dawn, shining brighter and brighter until midday" (Prov. 4:18).

Over the last forty years of tumultuous change, as the world shifted from the modern to the postmodern era, the church has taken its fair share of hits. What was once culturally accepted as a Christian norm in the West has shifted dramatically. The church has found itself outside the cultural mainstream. Many believers have had a difficult time understanding this massive shift from a Judeo-Christian society to a post-Christian, pantheistic society. Instead of holding the place of respect in the community, churches have become more and more marginalized in our cities and towns. And instead of confronting the culture with the truth of the gospel, despite the changing societal winds, many churches and individual Christians have shut themselves behind the heavy wooden doors of the church, pretending that the world is still the same as it was in 1955 when Eisenhower was president of the United States.

I have often said, "Cynicism is redundant." We already know what the problems are—anyone with intelligence can see the difficulties we face in the world today. We don't need people who think they are smarter than everyone else telling us what is wrong.

Instead we need visionaries who have the audacity to take God at His Word, to believe that "those who the Son sets free are free indeed" (John 8:36) to seek Him for the answers to the problems that face mankind, and to go to work among lost and hurting people to make a difference in this world.

For each believer today, it is imperative that we ask, is it the sunset, or the dawn?

It is time for the church to stop complaining, whining, and wallowing in self-pity and instead move out in the anointing, energy, provision, protection, and creativity that is ours both through the Edenic Covenant—"Let Us make man in Our image" and "they will rule" (Gen. 1:26)—and also the New Covenant in Christ—"All authority has been given to Me . . . Go, therefore, and make disciples of all nations" (Matt. 28:18–19).

Ronald Reagan and Pope John Paul II will go down in history as the men who through the casting of vision on the one hand, and the constant implementation of political pressure on the other, helped to bring down the Berlin Wall and collapse Communism in Europe. Not long before the end of his presidency, and before the end of the Cold War, Reagan gave students at Moscow University a preview of what was coming on the earth when he said, "Like a chrysalis, we're emerging from the economy of the industrial revolution—an economy confined to and limited by the earth's physical resources—into the economy of the mind, an era in which there are no bounds on human imagination and the freedom to create is the most precious natural resource."[6]

Across the globe we are seeing hopeful signs, even amid the dangers of militant Islam and Hinduism, even amid the strongholds of false religions in Asia and Africa, even amidst the stronghold of secularism in Europe and America. Across the world the religious walls are coming down, making way for the gospel to be preached to all people groups. Technology is making it possible for the Good News and Judeo-Christian cultural ideas to be spread through the Internet, mobile digital media, satellite television, radio, and print communication.

Contemporary travel allows people to move quickly across the globe and to see the wonders of the world—to be exposed to new ideas and to the freedom that comes through biblical truth, the Christian lifestyle, and Judeo-Christian ideas.

There is a historical shift of nations toward democracy and the corresponding freedoms of conscience, the press, and religion. People who encounter these ideas are no longer willing to be kept in religious and political prisons. New winds of freedom are blowing, and mankind is shaking off the shackles of secularism, communism, false religion, and totalitarian government.

Modern medicine and clean water are curbing the spread of diseases. Modern farming and food preservation techniques are eliminating hunger in most of the world.

E. Calvin Beisner points out that "on the average people produce more than they consume in their lifetimes. That is why growing human populations, far from threatening to create poverty and to exhaust natural resources, promise instead to create wealth and to multiply resources. Remember this: on the average, every mouth born into this world is attached to two hands—and, more important, to a mind made in the image of God to be creative and productive. That is why wealth is increasing."[7]

In the groundbreaking book *Discipling Nations*, Darrow Miller comments on Romans 8:19–22: "The creation waits in eager expectation for the sons of God to be revealed. For the creation was subjected to frustration, not by its own choice, but by the will of the one who subjected it, in hope that the creation itself will be liberated from its bondage to decay and brought into the glorious freedom of the children of God. We know that the whole creation has been groaning as in the pains of childbirth right up to the present time."

Miller gives this optimistic interpretation. "Here we learn several critical facts: (1) creation's fate and ours are inextricably bound together; (2) God's work of restoring all things to Himself is a process, a story, that will one day be consummated; (3) man has been commissioned to be a part of that process; and, by extension (4) science and technology are tools in this process."[8]

I couldn't agree more.

I don't think it's getting darker and darker in the world and that the devil is alive and well on planet Earth. I agree with Larry Tomczak's observation, "The devil may be alive, but he's not doing well. In fact, he knows his time is short."[9]

The Convergence of Technology, Communication, and Faith

All indications are that we are at a dramatic crossroads at the dawn of this new millennium—and much of the impetus for this revolution can be connected to the opening of conversations worldwide through the Internet.

Now is the time for the church to rise up into its proper place of dominion and creativity—believing God for strategies to reach the nations with the gospel so that all may know of God's plan of salvation. Jesus said, "the Kingdom of God suffers violence and those who take it, take it by force" (Matt. 11:12). It is time for the Church to take possession of all that has been promised to us and like Caleb said to Joshua, declare that, "We're as strong today as when God promised this land to us, so give to us this mountain!" (Josh, 14:11–12, author paraphrase).

In Christ and for the church and the world, using the dynamic tools on the Internet and through digital technology, I believe the best is yet to come!

NetCasters, arise and go forth—your day has come!

MORE FROM CRAIG VON BUSECK

Craig von Buseck on Facebook:
http://www.facebook.com/craigvonbuseck

www.vonbuseck.com

Craig's blog on CBN.com, updated weekdays:
http://blogs.cbn.com/ChurchWatch/

Craig's articles and interviews on CBN.com:
http://www.cbn.com/about/bios/craigvonbuseck.aspx

NOTES

Chapter 1

1. Internet World Stats, see http://www.Internetworldstats.com/stats.htm.

2. Internet World Stats, see http://www.Internetworldstats.com/stats.htm.

3. See http://www.alexa.com/topsites.

4 See http://www.reuters.com/article/internetNews/idUSN0559828420071106.

5. See http://www.email-marketing-reports.com/metrics/email-statistics.htm.

6. Pew Internet "Faith Online," see http://www.pewtrusts.org/uploadedFiles/wwwpewtrustsorg/News/Press_Releases/Society_and_the_Internet/pew_Internet_faith_0404.pdf.

7. Ibid.

8. See http://www.hitgeist.com.

9. See http://www.techcrunch.com/2009/06/04/the-true-value-of-social-networks-the-2009-updated-model.

10. R. Hauben, and H. M. Hauben, "A Brief History of the Internet," 1998, see http://www.columbia.edu/~rh120/other/birth_Internet.txt.

11. Pew Internet and American Life Project, "64% of Online Americans Have Used the Internet for Spiritual or Religious Purposes," see http://www.pewtrusts.org/news_room_ektid22636.aspx.

12. Barna Research, "More Americans Are Seeking Net-Based Faith Experiences," see http://www.barna.org/FlexPage.aspx?Page=BarnaUpdate&BarnaUpdateID=90.

13. Heidi Campbell, see http://www.stripes.com/article.asp?section=104&article=62813&archive=true.

14. Reggie McNeal, *The Present Future* (San Francisco, CA: Jossey-Bass, 2003).

15. William Gates, Nathan Myhrvold, and Peter Rinearson, *The Road Ahead* (New York, NY: Penguin Books, 1999), 11.

16. Tony Whittaker, "Online Evangelism," Web Evangelism Guide, see http://www.web-evangelism.com and http://guide.gospelcom.net.

17. Leonard Sweet, *Carpe Manana* (Grand Rapids, MI: Zondervan, 2003), 24.

Chapter 2

1. John Stott, "The Living God Is a Missionary God" found in *Perspectives on the World Christian Movement*, Revised Edition, edited by Ralph D. Winter and Steven C. Hawthorn (Pasadena, CA: The Institute of International Studies, William Carey Library, 1992), A10.

2. Ibid., A14.

3. Gordon Robertson, *Miracle Living Today Magazine*, Spring 2007, 12.

4. Bill Hamon, *The Eternal Church* (Santa Rosa Beach, CA: Christian International Ministries, 1995), 126.

5. Giles Wilson, "The Most Watched Film in History," see http://news.bbc.co.uk/1/hi/magazine/3076809.stm.

6. Allan Beeber, "How is Evangelism Changing in the 21st Century" *Internet Evangelism in the 21st Century: A Reader* (Handclasp International, edited by Dan Henrich), see http://pacrimmedia.files.wordpress.com, 22.

7. J. Gordon Melton, *Religious Leaders in America* (Farmington Hills, MI: Gale Publishing, 1999).

8. Pat Robertson, *Shout It From the Housetops* (Alachua, FL: Bridge Publishers, 1986), 148–49.

9. Allan Beeber, "How Is Evangelism Changing in the 21st Century?" *Internet Evangelism in the 21st Century: A Reader.*

10. Sterling Huston, "Internet Evangelism," *Internet Evangelism in the 21st Century: A Reader* (Handclasp International, 2007), edited by Dan Henrich.

11. *Ibid.*

Chapter 3

1. Lev Grossman, "You, Yes You, Are Time's Person of the Year," *Time*, see http://www.time.com/time/magazine/article/0,9171,1570810,00.html.

2 Internet World Stats, see http://www.Internetworldstats.com/stats.htm.

3. Tony Whittaker, Web Evangelism Guide, 2007, see http://www.web-evangelism.com.

4. John Edmiston, Internet Evangelism Conference, Chicago, IL, September, 2005.

5. Walt Wilson, Internet Evangelism Conference, Chicago, IL, September, 2005.

6. Don Tapscott and Anthony D. Williams, *Wikinomics: How Mass Collaboration Changes Everything* (New York, NY: Portfolio/Penguin, 2006), 37–38.

7. Tim O'Reilly, "What is Web 2.0?" see http://www.oreilly.com/pub/a/oreilly/tim/news/2005/09/30/what-is-Web-20.html.

8. Church Solutions, "Just What Is Web 2.0?" see http://www.churchsolutionsmag.com/articles/791cover0.html.

9. Kevin Hendricks, "The 21st Century Potluck: Web 2.0 and the Church," *Collide Magazine,* Issue 01, September, 2007, 48–49.

10. SlideShare, "Web 2.What?" see http://whitepapers.zdnet.co.uk/0,1000 000652,260287863p,00.htm?dl=1.

11. Charles Leadbeater, *We-Think* (London: Profile Books, 2009).

12. Tony Whittaker, Web Evangelism Guide, 2007, see http://www.web-evangelism.com.

13. Walt Wilson, Internet Evangelism Conference, Chicago, IL, September, 2005.

14. Haydn Shaughnessy, "What Will You See Next?" see http://www.mediangler.com/2006/10/03/at-last-the-last-content-types.

15. Church Solutions, "Just What Is Web 2.0?" see http://www.churchsolutionsmag.com/articles/791cover0.html.

Chapter 4

1. Søren Kierkegaard, *The Point of View*, ed. by Howard V. Hong and Edna H. Hong (Princeton, NJ: Princeton University Press, 1998), 45.

2. Tony Whittaker, "The Gray Matrix," see http://www.internetevangelismday.com/gray-matrix.php.

3. Ibid.

4. Mikael Andreasen, *Before I Close My Eyes: True E-mail Conversations of Faith and the Meaning of Life* (Grand Rapids,MI: Kregel Publishers, 2006).

5. Drew Dickens interview with the author.

6. Greg Outlaw, "Reaching the Connected Generation with Blogging," in *Internet Evangelism in the 21st Century,* edited by Dan Henrich, 56–57.

7. Karen Schenk, "Reaching the Connected Generation with Blogging," in *Internet Evangelism in the 21st Century* edited by Dan Henrich, 38.

8. Stephen Shields, "Reaching the Connected Generation with Blogging," in *Internet Evangelism in the 21st Century* edited by Dan Henrich, 169.

9. See http://www.sifry.com/alerts/archives/000493.html.

10. Stephen Shields, "Reaching the Connected Generation with Blogging," in *Internet Evangelism in the 21st Century* edited by Dan Henrich, 168.

11. Will Sampson, "Reaching the Connected Generation with Blogging," in *Internet Evangelism in the 21st Century* edited by Dan Henrich, 164.

12. Nick Ciske, "Reaching the Connected Generation with Blogging," in *Internet Evangelism in the 21st Century* edited by Dan Henrich, 164.

13. D. J. Chuang, "Reaching the Connected Generation with Blogging," in *Internet Evangelism in the 21st Century* edited by Dan Henrich, 166.

14. Steve Knight, "Reaching the Connected Generation with Blogging," in *Internet Evangelism in the 21st Century* edited by Dan Henrich, 167.

15. Michael Parsons, quoted in "The Death of Blogs" by Ted Olsen, *Christianity Today,y* September 25, 2007, see http://www.christianitytoday.com/ct/2007/october/13.22.html.

16. See LifeChurch.TV, "History of LifeChurch.tv," see http://www.lifechurch.tv/p/735/Default.aspx.

17. "About Us," Flamingo Road Church, see http://www.flamingoroadchurch.com/about.

Chapter 5

1 See http://www.latimes.com/business/la-fi-online-tv9-2009sep09,0,3144574.story.

2. Reuters, "Bill Gates: Internet Will Revolutionize Television," see http://www.foxnews.com/story/0,2933,248242,00.html.

3. Reuters, Bill Gates, January 2007.

4. See http://www.emarketer.com/Article.aspx?R=1007111.

5. Emarketer, "U.S. Country Overview," October 2007.

6. Alexander Castro, "eView: The Next Great Leap Forward for Web Video," see http://www.emarketingandcommerce.com/story/eview-next-great-leap-forward-Web-video.

7. Paul Verna, "Heard the Latest About Podcasting?" e-Marketer, February 4, 2008, see http://www.emarketer.com/Article.aspx?id=1005869&src=article1_newsltr.

8. Ibid.

9. Tony Whittaker interview with the author.

10. Jesse Carey interview with the author.

Chapter 6

1. Pew Internet and American Life Project, Teens and Social Media, Dec.19, 2007, see http://www.pewInternet.org/PPF/r/230/report_display.asp.

2. "Social Networking Online," Internet Evangelism Day with Tony Whittaker, see http://www.internetevangelismday.com/social-networking .php.

3. See http://www.cnn.com/2009/TECH/04/17/ashton.cnn.twitter.battle/index.html?iref=newssearch.

4. See http://www.scripting.com/stories/2007/07/27/whatTwitterIs.html.

5. "An Online Tragedy," 48 Hours-CBS News, www.cbsnews.com.

Chapter 7

1. See www.internetevangelismday.com/bridge-strategy.php.

2. "Search Engine Optimization," PCMag.com E-cyclopedia, see http://www.pcmag.com/encyclopedia_term/0%2C2542%2Ct%3Dsearch+engine+optimization&i%3D50995%2C00.asp.

3. Tiffany Maleshetski, "Code to Text Ratio," SEO Tools, see http://www.seochat.com/seo-tools/code-to-text-ratio.

4. Alan Beeber, "How is Evangelism Changing in the 21st Century?" in *Internet Evangelism in the 21st Century: A Reader* edited by Dan Henrich, 26.

Chapter 8

1. Barna, George. "The Year's Most Intriguing Findings, From Barna Research Studies," *The Barna Update*, December 17, 2001, see http://www.barna.org/FlexPage.aspx?Page=BarnaUpdate&BarnaUpdateID=103.

2. See http://www.sandykulkin.com.

3. Christianity Today, "Go Figure," see http://www.christianitytoday.com/ct/2007/june/4.20.html.

4. Gallup Organization Poll on Religion, see http://www.gallup.com/poll/1690/Religion.aspx.

5. Pew Internet "Faith Online," see http://www.pewtrusts.org/uploadedFiles/wwwpewtrustsorg/News/Press_Releases/Society_and_the _Internet/pew_Internet_faith_0404.pdf.

6. Baylor University. *American Piety in the 21st Century*, 2006, see http://www.baylor.edu/content/services/document.php/33304.pdf.

7. Lifeway Research (2007), see http://www.lifeway.com/lwc/article_main_page/0%2C1703%2CA%25253D165949%252526M%25253D200906%2C00.html?.

8. Sam S. Rainer, *Three Myths about Church Dropouts*, 2008, see http://samrainer.wordpress.com/2007/12/16/three-myths-about-church-dropouts.

Chapter 9

1. See www.internetevangelismday.com/vacancies.php.

Chapter 10

1. See www.lausanne.org.

Chapter 11

1. John Edmiston, IEC 2005 Annual Meeting Report, see http://www.webevangelism.com/newsletters/iecnewsletter-0905.html.

Chapter 12

1. Tony Whittaker, "The Web: A Unique Medium," *Internet Evangelism Day*, see http://www.internetevangelismday.com/medium.php.

2. Leonard Sweet, *Carpe Manana* (Grand Rapids, MI: Zondervan, 2003), 24.

3. Ibid.

4. Randy Komisar and Kent L. Lineback, *The Monk and the Riddle: The Art of Creating a Life While Making a Living*, (Boston, MA: Harvard Business School Press, 2001), 75.

5. Charles Spurgeon, *Sermons of the Rev. C. H. Spurgeon of London*, Seventh Series, sermon #349 (New York: Sheldon & Company, 1864), see http://www.cqod.com/index-06-23-07.html.

6. Steven F. Hayward, *The Age of Reagan* (New York: CrownForum, 2009), 606.

7. E. Calvin Beisner "Is There an Invisible Hand to Help the Poor?" *Crosswinds: The Reformation Digest*, Fall/Winter 1994–95, 51.

8. Darrow Miller, *Discipling Nations* (Seattle, WA: YWAM Publishing, 1998), 229.

9. Larry Tomczak, "Biblical Confessions to Build Your Faith," see http://resourcesforchristians.net/downloads/print/Biblical%20confessions%20to%20build%20your%20faith.doc, (accessed February 2010).